In the Land of the Willing

In the Land of the Willing

Litanies, Prayers, Poems, and Benedictions

Kenneth L. Sehested

Foreword by
Walter Brueggemann

RESOURCE *Publications* · Eugene, Oregon

IN THE LAND OF THE WILLING
Litanies, Prayers, Poems, and Benedictions

Copyright © 2014 Kenneth L. Sehested. All rights reserved. Except for brief quotations in critical publications or reviews, no part of this book may be reproduced in any manner without prior written permission from the publisher. Write: Permissions. Wipf and Stock Publishers, 199 W. 8th Ave., Suite 3, Eugene, OR 97401.

Resource Publications
An Imprint of Wipf and Stock Publishers
199 W. 8th Ave., Suite 3
Eugene, OR 97401

www.wipfandstock.com

ISBN 13: 978-1-4982-0036-3

Manufactured in the U.S.A.   10/23/2014

Grateful acknowledgment is made to the following for permission to reprint previously published material:

"Sorry, sorry, sorry," originally published in the online journal "The Progressive Christian," November 12, 2010, reprinted in Fellowship: A Magazine Of Peacemaking, published by the Fellowship of Reconciliation, Summer 2012, Vol. 77, No. 4–6.

"The new deuteronomist" was originally published as "The Deuteronomist" at www.ReadTheSpirit.com, an online magazine covering religion, spirituality, values, and interfaith and cross-cultural issues.

"Water of life: a baptismal prayer," co-written with Nancy H. Sehested, was originally published in *For the Living of These Days: Resources for Enriching Worship*," C. Michael Hawn, ed. (Macon, GA: Smyth & Helwys, 1995), 58.

"John the baptizer," "Easter's aftermath," "Ordinary time rocks," and "Invitation to spiritual shoppers" were originally published in *From the Psalms to the Cloud: Connecting to the Digital Age*, Maria Mankin and Maren C. Tirabassi, ed. (Cleveland: The Pilgrim Press, 2013), 109–110, 119, 121, 143. All rights reserved.

"This canyon of bleached bones" was originally published as "Breathe on us" in *Before the Amen: Creative Resources for Worship*, Maren C. Tirabassi and Maria I. Tirabassi (Cleveland: The Pilgrim Press, 2007), 226–227. All rights reserved.

"How dare the sun ascend" is reprinted with permission from *Sojourners Magazine*, November 2011.

Unless otherwise noted, Scripture quotations and references are from the New Revised Standard Version Bible, copyright 1989, Division of Christian Education of the National Council of the Churches of Christ in the United States of America. Used by permission. All rights reserved.

The Scripture quotation from THE MESSAGE. Copyright © by Eugene H. Peterson 1993, 1994, 1995, 1996, 2000, 2001, 2002. Used by permission of Tyndale House Publishers, Inc.

Glenda Jo Sehested
23 May 1948 – 29 April 2013
whose repeated refrain at
Augustana College,
Sioux Falls, South Dakota,
where she taught all her life, was
"We must continually wrestle
with questions of moral value."

Oh who will come and go with me....
"On Jordan's Stormy Banks"

Lyrics by Samuel Stennett (1787), music by Miss M. Durham, arr. by Rigdon M. McIntosh. The song crossed into popular culture with Johnny Cash's 2003 rendition under the title of "I Am Bound for the Promised Land."

Contents

Foreword by Walter Brueggemann | xi
Preface | xiii
Acknowledgments | xv
Introduction | xvii

The Calling
In the land of the willing | 1

I Hindrance & Desert
Anointed | 5
The Prophet's lament | 6
Come into the desert | 7
Kindle slavery's funeral pyre | 8
Dry bones | 9
Mutinous lips | 10
The boundary of bedlam | 11
Cheek to cheek | 12
Instruction on freedom's demands | 13
Take heed | 14
Oh foofaraw | 15
A plan for displacement | 16
Demoniac | 17
By the Beautiful Gate | 18
Bread and breast of Heaven | 20
Spiritual shoppers | 21
Blessed unrest | 22
Abiding in the shadow | 23

Contents

II Mercy

Amnesty | 27
Unimagined grace | 28
Maître d' of Heaven | 29
Mercy's requite | 30
Sired in mercy | 31
The payback of Heaven | 32
Reverent ovation and wonder's avail | 33
Let gladness swell your heart | 34
By Thy might | 35
Love of Christ | 36
Samaritan woman | 37
Let the lost rejoice | 38
Celebrant of mercy | 39

III Transformation

By the Word of Truth | 43
Riff on Isaiah five-eight | 44
This canyon of bleached bones | 45
Getting in the way | 46
That friggin' Lexus | 47
Sister Anna | 48
John the baptizer | 49
Too big for their britches | 50
The meek shall inherit the earth | 51
Morning by morning | 52
Easter's aftermath | 53
Keep it real | 55
Pace yourself | 56
Faith without fanfare | 57
Ordinary time rocks | 58
Life transfigured | 60
Bodies in gear | 61
The new deuteronomist | 62
Would that you knew | 63
Blistering hope | 64

IV Praise & Thanksgiving

On saying thanks | 69
Breath of Heaven | 71
The work of praise | 72
With courage impart | 75
Weeping may linger | 76
Widow woman | 77
Sip of joy | 78
The ministry of encouragement | 79
When you call I will answer | 81
Big band or bluegrass | 82
Holy Great Smokies | 83
Allahu Akbar | 86

V Songs

A Mighty Fortress Is Our God | 89
Abide With Me | 89
All People That On Earth Do Dwell | 90
Amazing Grace | 91
Beatitudes | 91
Breathe On Me, Breath of God | 92
Christ the Lord is Risen Today | 93
Doxology | 93
For All the Saints | 94
God Be With You Till We Meet Again | 95
How Can I Keep From Singing | 96
Lead On, O King Eternal | 96
Let All Mortal Flesh Keep Silent | 97
Now the Day Is Over | 97
O Come, O Come, Emmanuel | 98
O Little Town of Bethlehem | 99
Precious Lord | 99
This Is My Song | 100

Contents

VI Occasional

Litany for Martin Luther King, Jr. Day | 103
The earth is the Lord's | 105
Poisoned sea, impoverished soul | 107
The octopus, too | 109
All Saints' Day | 110
Come home | 111
Advent longing | 112
Boundary to benedictus | 114
Joseph | 116
The manger's reach | 118
Sorry, sorry, sorry | 120
Limb by limb | 122
Building a culture of peace | 124
A Christian-Muslim call to worship | 126
Ordination invocation | 128
Water of life: a baptismal prayer | 130
Ten years | 132
Acquainted with grief | 133
How dare the sun ascend | 134
The breadth of Heaven's reach | 136
Let the banquet begin | 137

VII Benedictus

Lean toward the land | 141
House of meeting | 142
Go out in joy | 143
The last word: a wedding blessing | 144
For that Bright Land | 146
Blessings, benedictions, and charges | 147

Scripture reference index | 153

Foreword

In his instruction to his disciples, Jesus declares: "Therefore every scribe who has been trained for the kingdom of Heaven is like the master of a household who brings out of his treasure what is new and what is old" (Matthew 13:52).

Well, Ken Sehested is exactly that kind of scribe. He has in his treasure "what is old." Ken is scripture-saturated. He knows the biblical texts so well that these simply arise when he wants to say something. He has an unerring sensibility for the nuance of the text, and for finding the right text at the right time.

But this is no dull reiteration of the text; he has in his treasure "what is new." What is new with Ken are many new words in poetic idiom that flow from the biblical text. As a result, he can mobilize the great hymns of the church, but does so with rich variation and puckish revision.

The outcome of that blend of what is old and what is new is a rich awareness of how the world is around us, a devoted awareness of the heritage and vocation of the church, and a resolve to be honest about the church and the world in the presence of the gospel.

Readers will promptly see that this is the work of one who is "trained for the kingdom of Heaven." And when readers are attentive and engage in his lyrical offer, they will find themselves as well "trained for the kingdom," attuned to the new governance of God that requires fresh, imaginative obedience. This book is a great gift to us; it issues in a calling that befits the coming rule of God.

>   Walter Brueggemann
>   Columbia Theological Seminary
>   June 4, 2014

Preface

Much of the material that follows was originally written for use in my own congregation. Many from here and from my earlier book, *In the Land of the Living*, can be found at my online journal and blog, *prayerandpolitiks.org*, which is frequently updated.

    Local congregations may occasionally use this material, as is or in edited form, without permission. For regular use, contact Wipf & Stock for permission.

    Many of these compositions were written expressly for worship in response to particular biblical texts—usually one or more of the lectionary texts for the week. In some places I have simply paraphrased or adapted the text. More often I've latched on to evocative words, phrases or themes, and turned my imagination loose. (Thus the "inspired by" notation at the end of most of these prayers.) Never to supplant the text, of course, but only to allow its dynamism a chance to interpret current realities. Such writing is not unlike the Jewish Midrashic tradition of commentary.

    My highest hope is that these offerings will inspire you to write your own prayers for personal and corporate use. I can attest that the weekly composition discipline is itself a potent form of prayer.

Acknowledgments

Abigail Hastings was the creative genius who gave shape to a pile of poems, weeding out the stragglers, cutting the fat, finding the proper outline and order, even coming up with the title, creating continuity with my previous book of litanies, *In the Land of the Living*. That she is an in-law is an added bonus for me. Her own writing is available at my online journal and blog, *prayerandpolitiks.org*.

Julie Lonneman's cover art is revelatory and provides artistic continuity with my previous work. You can find her work at many places on the web, and she blogs at *julielonneman.blogspot.com*.

My pastoral colleague and freelance author/retreat leader Joyce Hollyday donated her professional proofreading skills to rid this work of blemishes as well as surfacing, in the process, numerous copyediting questions needing attention.

My good friend and fellow church member Dale Roberts, who has guided many a college student in discerning vocation, did the tedious work of confirming the accuracy of the numerous Scripture references.

Members of Circle of Mercy Congregation in Asheville, North Carolina, were the first to receive and respond to much of this material. Their encouragement has been invaluable. Under the banner of *seeking justice, pursuing peace, and following Jesus*, we together continue exploring the rule of mercy in all things, through seasons of bounty and of limit, in and out of ease, whether surprised by joy or bruised by sorrow, ever *leaning on the everlasting arms*

Introduction

In my previous collection of offerings for personal prayer and public liturgy, the title *In the Land of the Living* came from the shockingly materialistic affirmation of the psalmist: "I believe that I shall see the goodness of the Lord *in the land of the living.*" (Psalm 27:13, emphasis added).

By *materialist* I do not mean the kind of reductionism that characterizes elements of modern science—quantum physicists have pulled the rug out from under that dogmatism. My claim, rather, is that any spirituality that does not take *stuff* seriously is seriously deficient. It is hollow, "holding to the outward form of godliness but denying its power." (2 Tim 3:5) It leads to ingrown souls.

The purpose of this volume is to continue and expand my earlier work in articulating an alternative theological vision to those self-referencing, often narcissistic practices that pass for *spirituality,* whether of the increasingly anemic traditional kind or the ethereal newer-age variety.

My testimony continues to be this: God is more taken with the agony of the earth than with the ecstasy of Heaven. The Spirit traffics in earthly affairs. And when we undertake spiritual disciplines (centering prayer, for instance), the center to which our prayer calls us will likely be smack dab in the middle of the world's decentered, disoriented, disabled, and dysfunctional life.

The resolve of God's love is not for redemption in the time beyond time, in a place beyond the farthest galaxy, but precisely in and through this time, this space, in and through the tear-stained, blood-smeared, history-happening world. The Incarnation, our confession's most distinctive claim, is not an anecdote of God holding Heaven's nose to be lowered into *temporal* sewage in order to rescue for *eternity* a few who've managed to crawl out of the muck.

Rather, the turn toward God entails a turning toward the Beloved's vision for creation—for the world, before it became *worldly.* Thus the joy of that beatific vision baptizes us into grief and lament at what the world has become. Ironically, our capacity to grieve and lament is directly related to our capacity for hope, for our confidence in the trustworthiness of that

Introduction

vision—much like the circumference of a tree's trunk and the reach of its limbs—is proportionate to its root system.

This is what we do in worship, where grief is mixed with grace and offered up as praise, not for another world but for the renewal of that Wind that first hovered over the chaos and the Word that gave shape to creation. Such praise—doxology, in fertile times and in famine—functions as both promise and provocation. The recognition of majesty and the work of mercy (in its largest sense, not merely charity) are irrevocably bound, each nourishing and informing and enabling the other.

Mercy

In these pages *mercy* is a prominent theme and a repeated refrain.

When two colleagues and I began Circle of Mercy Congregation in Advent 2001, we quickly came to agreement (for a variety of overlapping reasons) that both words, circle and mercy, needed to be in our name. After a year or so together, our congregation further clarified its vision through extended conversations about a motto or byword. Eventually we reached consensus on a tripartite phrase: *seeking justice, pursuing peace, following Jesus.*

My principal reason for wanting *mercy* in our name is because the word represents the agency which mediates the prerequisites of peace with the demands of justice. On its own, the clamor for peace easily lends itself to accommodation with oppression and passivity in the face of violence. (As one military dictator commented, when asked if he would offer peace terms to rebel forces, "I will give them the peace of the sepulcher.") Likewise, an exclusive insistence on justice readily devolves into vengeance and retaliation. (As Gandhi wrote, "An eye for an eye makes the whole world blind.")

Following Jesus (rather than merely *believing in Jesus*) is our preferred vocabulary of allegiance, because we believe that any serious conversation about Jesus is transacted on the road, in concrete acts of seeking justice and pursuing peace, with everything we do constantly mediated by the vigilant rule of mercy. Spirituality incites work that will raise calluses, sometimes blisters. Bloody noses, sometimes worse, are not out of the question.

What we experience in such engagements, whether with hopeful or discouraging results (both happen on a regular basis), feeds our liturgy, giving voice both to joy and grief, hallelujahs and heartaches, in experienced measure—all of which, taken together, conspire to undermine the rule of every empire.

Introduction

Of course, the empire will strike back and send us, again, to our knees. In that posture we are pushed to pray more deeply, beyond the calculus of our own competence, and soaked again by the invocation of a new Heaven and a new earth (Isa 66:22; Rev 21:1), then rising anew to pursue ever more vigorously the things that make for peace. (Luke 19:42) And on it goes, prayer prompting a *realpolitik* of the Spirit, the bruises of which shepherd us back into deepening prayer, each pursuit leavening the other, creating a sustainable ecology of hope.

Of these three—faith, hope and love (1 Cor 13:13)—love is the greatest, but hope may be the hardest.

Perseverance

Another theme in the pages that follow reflects our congregation's learned experience over the years. Through our own failures, our sluggish seasons, our inspiration-gone-sour moments, we have seen that *faithful persistence* may be the most recurring and insistent testimony of Scripture, where God's *steadfast love* is prominent.

Legendary singer-songwriter-activist Pete Seeger (blessed be his memory) spoke of *defiant optimism*. (He was the inspiration for a movement to clean up the southern end of the Hudson River, so long used as a cesspool by the metropolitan New York City region. He liked to say, "We did it with our little teaspoons.") German theologian Dorothee Sölle (also of blessed memory) spoke of *revolutionary patience*. A half-century ago a theological movement based in Brazil, living under a brutal military dictatorship, gathered around the phrase *firmeza permanente,* roughly translated as *relentless firmness* or active nonviolence characterized by courage and resolve.

In a culture where spirituality is often little more than thrill-seeking voyeurism and religious tourism, perseverance is a thing of homegrown beauty.

So we keep showing up—for worship and study, for praying and for playing—like a gardener who patiently plants, waters, weeds, and waits. Preoccupations, however brilliant; goals and objectives, however well-crafted; programs

Introduction

and priorities, however well-intentioned—all these are subject to decay. Repentance is a practice, not an accomplishment. Perseverance, especially when moods languish, is essential, for no one can predict when Pentecost's fire may again alight and the gusty wind return.

When it does, often from an unexpected direction, we are prone to catch courage from each other. And we find ourselves, again, refreshed *in the land of the willing.*

>Kenneth L. Sehested
>Ordinary Time 2014

The Calling

In the land of the willing

This is one of those
old-fashioned, free-range,
leap-of-faith callings.
Just when you thought
our climate-controlled,
pension-secured culture
had squeezed all the
chutzpah out of the
believing community —
no more burning bushes,
flaming tongues-of-fire,
scary angelic appearances,
even still-small voices —
the Spirit erupts again
for those with ears to hear
and hearts aligned.

*A blessing for friends prior to their year
teaching and being taught by the church in Cuba.*

I Hindrance & Desert

Anointed

Do not say with your lips, "The Spirit of the Lord!
The Spirit of the Lord!" when your hearts are
    shackled in fear, enslaved to security.

The spirit of the Lord God is upon me,
    because the Lord has anointed.

Anointed you for what?!
Have you grown confused by
    the barking of market reports?
By the demands of national security?
By your 401(k) addiction?

Anointed to bring good news to the oppressed,
    to bind up the brokenhearted.

"The Spirit of the Lord! The Spirit of the Lord!"
Your comfort-conditioned prayers leave little room
    for the Spirit's work of seeing the world from below.

Anointed to proclaim the captives' release, sight
    to the blind, freedom to every bonded body.

Can you not see? "The Spirit of the Lord" breaks forth
    from the ash heap, from the cells of incarcerated
    despair, from dispirited cries and discomforted eyes.

Now anoint us anew, and by grace comprehend,
    the Spirit's sure leading to the margin's amend.

Inspired by Isa 61:1–2 & Luke 4:18

The Prophet's lament

Doubtless one day you will have cause
to chant the Prophet's lament:

> *Truly,*
> *thou art a God*
> *who hidest thyself.*

Even so, I still prefer this One to the other,
more snuggly brand, who feigns intimacy

but has the aroma of cheap perfume,
cheaper wine and layered sweat,

having been passed around by too many
lusty barkers for whom ecstasy's aftermath
            is nauseous stupor.

∼ *Citing Isaiah 45:15* ∼

Come into the desert

The time has come to flee Pharaoh's national
security state for the insecurity of the wilderness.

Led by the Spirit and sustained by angels,
                      we head to the desert
            for a throw-down with the Devil.

Fear not. God will sustain you.
Your clothes will not wear out,
            your feet will not swell.

    And yet we tremble:

Why have you led us from the
       prosperous land of shopping
           and shiny plastic things
on this highway to the danger zone?

What could be wrong with harvesting bread from stones?
                              And a little Vegas-style magic?

Why not lay claim to all the world's kingdoms?
                          Wasn't Jesus "exceptional"?

And don't we, his followers, get a piece of that action?

Can God spread a table in the wilderness
            without Wall Street backing?

    Come into the desert, O people of Mercy,
to find the One whom your heart most desires.

∼ Inspired by Matt 4:1–11 & Deut 8:1–10. ∼

Kindle slavery's funeral pyre

By wind's pillar of cloud, by flame's column of fire,
do we live and move toward journey's unseen home.

We are coming from slavery, yet with bones grown
accustomed to Pharaoh's protection.

Whose memory shall we privilege;
    whose purpose confirm?

Whose story will be recited;
    whose providence trusted?

Can the bones of Joseph shield
    from empire's seductive reach?

Will the allure of indentured ease o'erpower
    the risk of freedom's appeal?

Wind's pillar by day, flame's column by night,
    guide hearts in this fray, scatter languishing fright.

Who will feed in the desert?
    Who will quench thirst's regret?

Can trembling bones be comforted?
    Shall crushed marrow rejoice?

Roar, you Pentecostal Wind! Alight,
    you tongues of fire!

Breach the bulwark of captive bondage.
    Kindle slavery's funeral pyre!

∽ Inspired by Exod 13:17–22 & the story of Pentecost in Acts 2 ∽

Dry bones

'Neath the canyons of vengeance
    lies the valley of bones.
Many bones. Dry bones.
Bleached by remorse and hope's demise.

Child of Eden's failure and Noah's fortune.
    Forsaken.
    Forgotten.
    Forlorn.

"Can these bones live?" asks the Lord of Hosts.
"Only you know," say our doubt-tendered lips.

"Prophesy, you raggedy-ann human!" came the reply.
"Prophesy to the wind. Demand Heaven's own Breath!"

Behold: comes the shaking, bone fit to bone.
Followed by sinews, knitting each to all.

"Say to these graves,
    'Your death grip has ended!
        Your rancor, exhausted;
            your redemption, sure purchased.'"

Then finally the flesh, like a dress of pure glory!

"Stand erect, resurrected. For your land
is prepared to receive its plow;
your soil, its seed; your table, its bounty."
The harvest of plenty awaits your delight.

Thus sayeth the Lord, flesh adoring;
bestowed by the Word, earth restoring.

～ Inspired by Ezek 37:1–14 ～

Mutinous lips

From the depths of distress, every sail sagged and limp,
my mutinous lips offer insurrecting sighs.

With heart-aching hope doth my voice still rejoice.
Incline us, consign us, to steadfast Embrace.

Fealty abandoned, no horizon in sight, my stride still
ascends the steep provident path.

With bone-bruising hope doth my voice still rejoice.
Incline us, consign us, to steadfast Embrace.

For I know that great stone, once rejected, now anchors
a mansion of welcome to both strangers and kin.

With feet-wearied hope doth my voice still rejoice.
Incline us, consign us, to steadfast Embrace.

With glad songs of vict'ry from the formerly vanquished,
let the festal procession loot the treasury of fear.

With soul-rested hope doth my voice still rejoice.
Incline us, consign us, to steadfast Embrace.

∼ Inspired by Ps 118 ∼

The boundary of bedlam

From the turbulent bowels of darkest deep,
    our roiling souls cry to you, O God!

Close not your ears to the sound of our
    afflictions! Remind us again that Heaven's
Provision will yet outlast earth's squalid distress.

Draw us to the Still Point of love's tranquil refrain,
    to the melody of restful hearts:

"Be still and know, still and know, know that I am God."

In our watching and waiting, on the
    Boundary of bedlam and the squalling,
        the brawling, the frivolous noise,
shield us from the Confuser's snare.

"Be still and know, still and know, know that I am God."

O people of Mercy,
    of promise and pardon,
        lean into the One
            who alone shall abide.

∼ Inspired by Ps 130 & Ps 46 ∼

Cheek to cheek

Thus says Yahweh, author and anchor of creation,
to the people of Promise whose memory has failed:

When you were but a babe, I cradled you. I swept you
into my arms and nestled you under my chin.

I suckled you and sang sweetly, cheek to cheek,
calming your restless hands and feet.

From Pharaoh's deadly bargain I purchased your release.
Why have you grown tired of my attention?

What beguiling voice has led you into this wanton,
wayward desert of destruction—back into the arms
of the empires of vanity and vengeance?

Shall I unleash my righteous wrath against you?
Can your trust be hinged on nothing but
Assyrian brute force?

Shall I now save you with my destructive anger?
Shall I release you to the pillage of national security?

Thus says the Most High and Holy One of Heaven:
My heart recoils at the thought of plundering you
in order to pardon you.

Instead, I will woo you. I will wait you out.

*(Do you yet seek me to utter? A clue—look
for my Presence among the clutter.)*

∽ *Inspired by Hos 11 & Matt 7:7–8* ∽

Instruction on freedom's demands

Abandon every god of metal:
    whether nation or spear or bandolier,
    each Tomahawk and Trident,
    every nuclear racketeer.
Do not sanction your vengeance by
    the Name of the Beloved.

Border the harvest of your production
    with fallow sabbath rest.
Not all of life can be monetized.

Honor your father from whose seed you now flourish;
hallow your mother, whose womb issued breath.

    Do no murder:
        Life is not yours to take.
    Don't stoop to infidelity:
        No body is available for frivolous consumption.
    Steal not:
        You'll destroy life's fabric.
    Slander not:
        You'll poison life's well.
    Covet not:
        Your own health is tied up with
        that of your neighbor.

Let not threat of sword nor promise of reward
    cause you to forget this holy accord.

For this, now, is your creed:
    Once slaved, now freed.
        As liberated from greed,
            by righteousness proceed.

~ Inspired by Exod 20 ~

Take heed

Take heed, all of you, that your possessions
do not choke the breath from your lungs,
rout the glee from your hands, or steal the
affection of your hearts.

The longing for more, and yet more,
and more again, grows faster
than kudzu, whose greenery—
though pleasant of sight—
smothers everything in its grasp.

Take heed, all of you, and resist the urge
for bigger barns and the impulse to secure
your life by the power of your own appetites.

The longing for more, and yet more, and more again,
will spoil your appetite for all that is truly good,
    all that is truly beautiful, all that truly satisfies.

Take heed, all of you, who have more than enough,
for your bounty and abundance will become a
burden and encumbrance.

The longing for more, and yet more,
    and more again,
will sever your relations: with each other,
        with the land,
            and with the Beloved One
who provides enough for our need (but not for our greed).

Sisters and brothers, your wanting is not flawed
if you long to be rich, be rich, be rich and yet more—
long to be rich in God!

   ∼ Inspired by Luke 12:13–21 ∼

Oh foofaraw

Dear God:
There was a time when your provision was like a splendid
feast, a delicacy for the eye, a delight to the palate,
    an aroma so fine it buckled my knees.

But no more.
The thrill is gone.
    The aroma gags.
        I've had my fill of this swill.

Bitter the word, broken the promise, that once
thrilled and fulfilled and instilled life with flavor.

What went wrong? I have not gone carousing
with the merchants of squalor.
    The mark of your Name, once a source of joy,
        now brands with scorn.
    The weight of your hand, once a source of comfort,
        now drags like a ball and chain.

My pain reeks, unceasing.
My wounds throb, relentless.
Your promise taunts
    like a desert mirage.
Your river of sustenance
    is swallowed in dust.

Oh, foofaraw, says the Beloved.
    Get over yourself! Your lips are flapping
        But your tongue's lost its nerve.

Turn and face me, if you dare not despair.
For the love of Christ, get a grip on your gripes.

    Inspired by Jer 15:16–19

A plan for displacement

The words of the Prophet Jeremiah,
sent from his perch among the ruins of Jerusalem,
to the priests and elders of Zion
    marched into Babylonian captivity.

Lift your hearts, you anxious exiles.
The Abiding One has tracked
    every sorrow-laden step.
The purpose of Providence has a plan
    for your displacement.

Build your houses with steadfast confidence.
Prepare for a harvest of hopeful delight.
Unleash your progeny with fertile resolve.
Seek the welfare of your transient home.

For I have planted you there with most
Holy Intent—not for harm or grievance,
but in new and inviolate covenant.

Be exiles no longer but citizens betrothed to
the outcaster's welfare now welcomed from afar.

Inhabit the land of apparent dismay.
    Register to vote,
        join the neighborhood watch,
            get yourself a library card
                and linger content.

Surely and surely the Sovereign's intent
        will uphold you,
           enfold you,
                in buoyant consent.

∼ Inspired by Jer 29:1–14 ∼

Demoniac

O Dispossessor of every possessed soul,
in our heart of hearts we beg you to leave us be.
Torment us no longer with your profligate mercy—
    serfs that we are to despondent pain.

By night and by day, amid the tombs' decay,
unrestrained, chained in vain:
        Our name be Legion.

Howling and heaving, mind ravaged with
grieving, body bruised and seething:
        Our name be Forlorn.

What do you have to do with us, Sweet Jesus,
prodigy of Heaven's affair with earth's wayward bent?

Still now. Be ever so still.
To your right mind requite,
    to your fold reunite,
        speak amazement's delight
            for the armistice declared.

∼ Inspired by Mark 5:1–20 ∼

By the Beautiful Gate

By the Beautiful Gate doth my heart lie abandoned,
confined to the dust by crippled estate, dependent on
shame for a shekel's remorse and a pitiful glance.

    Look at me,
if you dare to compare your lofty composure.

Season by season, we watch for the light of the sun's
promised rise and Messiah's awaited approach.
We long for redemption beyond silver and gold,
    beyond every imperial consent.

    Here Yeshua*
stumbled on his way to that hill, the judgment of those
with investments to guard.

    Here Stephen
was stoned for his wonders and signs, blaspheming the
beggar-filled temple's reproach.

    Season by season
we fancy a word from a John or a Peter, for some grace
overheard. We long for a gift
    beyond charity's rue,
    beyond silver and gold,
for the bounty of wonder;
    for a Presence divine,
        arrayed in full splendor.

By the Beautiful Gate

> *Look at us,*

the disciples demanded. Oh indigent soul, disabled of
limb and dishonored of heart, the Abling One comes
> with honor-laced eyes, causing feet to arise with
>> the high prize of praise.

> *Season by season*

by the Beautiful Gate—now plastered and bricked by
despair's brutal reign, we long for redemption
> beyond silver and gold,
>> beyond all imperial consent.

> *How long,*

how long shall predestined Mercy
lie tangled and tethered with grief?
> *How long,*

how long 'til gravity's sway shall
> relinquish its stay over feet made
>> for leaping and eyes for delight?

~ *Inspired by Acts 3:1–10* ~

*Transliteration of Jesus' Hebrew name.

Background: *The walls of the old city of Jerusalem bear seven gates. The oldest was known as the Beautiful Gate in Jesus' day, though its common name now is the Golden Gate. It is on the east wall, where the Shining Glory of God entered the city and where the Messiah was to be revealed.*

Archeologists believe the Beautiful Gate was built on the ruins of an older gate named the Mercy Gate. It was here that John and Peter encountered the crippled man begging for alms in the story from Acts 3. Legend has it that Jesus passed through this gate on his final entry into Jerusalem, and then was marched out this gate, carrying his cross on his way to crucifixion. Legend also has it that the Jewish-Christian community's first martyr, Stephen, was stoned in front of this gate. The gate was walled shut in the ninth-century and has remained so ever since.

Bread and breast of Heaven

The signal of Moses' ordination
erupted as bread, from the sky—
and water, from the rock—amid the
trackless and barren waste where
no tillage is found, no rivulet is formed.

> *Bread and Breast of Heaven,*
> *feed me 'til I want no more.*

Nourishment appears where none is
warranted, save by those who dare the
departure from Pharaoh's granary.
Save by those who abandon Moab's
drought and hopeless prospect to return,

like Naomi—accompanied in trust by
another without claim on the Promise—
to the place where God feeds.

> *Bread and Breast of Heaven,*
> *feed me 'til I want no more.*

Here God anoints with courage and
delight those with eyes to see, ears to
hear, and feet fit for the journey along
the blazed trail marked for those
without claim.

> *Bread and Breast of Heaven,*
> *feed me 'til I want no more.*

∾ Inspired by Exod 17:6 and the story of Naomi and Ruth in the book of Ruth. ∾

Spiritual shoppers

Attention,
all you spiritual shoppers.
There are no discounts. No sale prices.
No fifty percent off summer specials, no bonus miles,
no pre-inventory clearance or back-to-school savings.

There are no shortcuts to faith, no money-back
guarantees, no lifetime warranties or last-minute deals.

There are no wading pools. The depths are deep and
turbulence is standard. Every minute is your last.

If you want a God-soaked life, move to the margins.
Plant sequoias.* Find an eroded field and stake your
soul on its reclamation.

Synchronize your hope to an abandoned child's heartbeat.
Set your sights on the interest from millennial investments.

Say o'er the clamor of all merchandizing madness:
 Life is not had
 by what is possessed,
  but only by
what has been promised.**

~ *Inspired by Prov 29:18* ~

*Line from Wendell Berry, "Manifesto: The Mad Farmer Liberation Front," Collected Poems 1957–1982 (San Francisco: North Point Press, 1985), 151.
**Line from Walter Brueggemann, Living Toward a Vision (Madison, NJ: Shalom Resource Center, 1982), 124.

Blessed unrest

You who know little of
the underside of bridges,
the short side of markets,
the wrong side of the tracks
or the inside of jails.

The Holy One of Heaven
    is neither kindly uncle
        nor auntie sweet.

God is not "nice."
God is no lucky charm.
God is an earthquake.*

O Blessed Unrest,
disturb the peace
of the counsels of deceit.

Unnerve every
congress of infamy.
Shake the foundation
of all insular living.

Come and wrangle our hearts
with the dis-ease of your Love.

~ *Inspired by "God of Tempest, God of Whirlwind" by Herman Stuempfle, Jr.* ~

*The line is variously attributed to Rabbi Abraham Joshua Heschel, as a Yiddish proverb and as a saying from Hasidic Judaism.

Abiding in the shadow

Attend to my cry, O Lord; hide me in the
shadow of your wings.

Beloved One, my mouth praises you with
joyful lips; and in the shadow of your wings
my voice resounds.

"I will protect those who know my name,"
says the Strength of Day and the Guardian of Night.
"When they call me, then shall I answer."

Woe to you who take refuge in
    any freemarketer's dream,
    any warrior's scheme,
    any tyrant's regime.
Every militarized threat invites devastation;
every nuclear shadow casts unfolding destruction.

All again shall live 'neath my Shadow concealed:
flourishing, nourishing, succulent yield. By tenderful
mercy—O Dawn of High Heaven—break upon us,
redeem us from death-shadowed reign.

For succor and strength, confine to the Shadow;
there abide, reside, whatever betide.
In the fullness of time the Call will be sounded;
the pathway of peace, reveal and confide.

∽ Inspired by numerous biblical texts that mention "shadow," including Ps 17, 63, 91; Isa 30; Hos 14; Luke 1 ∽

II Mercy

Amnesty

If you, O God, should keep track of all our failures,
none of us would make the grade.

But your hands heap pardon on all the penitent.
Forgiveness is your middle name.
Mercy is your mandate; pardon, your provision.

Declarations of amnesty flow from your lips.
Every remorse is met with remission.

The feet of your grace rush to our incarcerated souls.

> *Oh restless, fitful hearts:*
Wait for your Redeemer;
> for the Word that unlocks prison doors,
> that infiltrates our enslaved minds.

~ *Inspired by Ps 130* ~

Unimagined grace

Stand amazed, you betrothed of unimagined Grace.
    Your siege is ending.

The Regent of Heaven shall come
    to reclaim the earth,
        to restore its shared inheritance,
    to redeem its memory of mercy
        and its generous harvest.

In those days the remnant of pardon will arrive
from every far-flung hill and hamlet.
    Among them will be the shamed and forsaken,
        the exposed and exploited; the blind and the lame
        and the laboring women.

A new day will break with stunning news: Wisdom's
    womb shall confound every weapon's contempt.

Disconsolate tears form streams of pure gladness.
    All shall approach without stumbling or regret.

My people will be known as a garden of plenty.
    Dancing shoes and festive attire will displace
        every mourner's ashen array.

From the least to the greatest, no sorrow, no sin,
    shall offend or rescind Heaven's ransomed delight.

∼ Inspired by Jer 31 ∼

Maître d' of Heaven

Elisha led the enemy to Israel's butchering floor.
But no blood was shed—instead, they were fed,
and they ransacked and raided no more.

Not even enemies are left to destitution,
nor the table of sinners refused.
The Beloved's steadfast love is like
a lip-smacking feast of abundance.

    "Food is not a weapon,"
Jesus answered Satan's bidding.
      Feasting is for mending,
          not for servitude and slavery.

The Maître d' of Heaven commands the
'poverished-poor to table: the halt and helpless,
lamed and maimed ushered up for honored seating.

Is it against the law to feed the immigrant?
Then join the jailhouse chorus
singing praise for God's provision!

The oil of plenty shall not fail
      the extravagant of soul.

Inspired by 2 Kgs 6:8–23; Zech 7:6–10; Matt 4:1–4

Mercy's requite

"I am but a child!" *you say.*
"What business do you have with people of no claim,
of no clout, of no clue about the road to repentance
and the return from exile?"

Aahh, oh clueless one, of no claim and no clout,
you know not that of which you speak!
Before your mother's maiden life, I knew you;
before your father's toddling feet,
I planned your sinews and mapped your countenance.

O child of consecrated lips and covenant voice,
    relinquish your fear!
        You shall not be put to shame.
            Your Refuge is secure.
It is you, oh child of destined grace,
    who will utter the Word that will shatter all enmity.

So let the nations tremble at the
    joy-filled cymbal-clapping songs
        of redemption's approach.

Let every wicked grip and cruelty's grasp
    be loosed by the grammar of praise.

No scorn, no disgrace, can ever erase
    the full pleasure of Mercy's requite.

Inspired by Jer 1:4–10 & Ps 71

Sired in mercy

Come to the Mercy Seat, to hear
the Word of gracious entreaty:
Life is more than bartered goods;
more still than hedged funds
        and market share.

Come to the Mercy Seat, to hear
the Word of gracious appeal:
Faith is more than philosophical posture;
        more still than fondling guarantee.

Come to the Mercy Seat, to hear
    the Word of gracious insistence:
Hope is more than risk aversion;
    more still than fingers crossed
        or fanciful dreaming.

Come to the Mercy Seat, to hear
the Word of gracious imperative:
Love is more than reciprocal affection;
    more still than curried favor
        or compounded interest.

Come to the Mercy Seat, to hear
the Word of gracious release:
You have been sired in Mercy
    and suckled in pardon;
        weaned on grace and
        restored by forgiveness.

Come to the Mercy Seat, for earth
has no sorrow that Heaven cannot heal.

Final phrase from the hymn "Come, Ye Disconsolate," Thomas Moore, alt. by Thomas Hastings.

The payback of Heaven

The payback of Heaven neither tortures nor torments.

The vengeance of God is Christ's victory of mercy,
o'er all venal indenture and vile deception.

The terror of God is the Risen One's threat
to every merchant of death, every marketer's breath,
every peddler of gun-wielding promise of power,

Whose assault is but aimed at the shame which
confounds and ensnares you.

Rise up with joy, every fleshly heart, to greet the
    One who entreats you;
Who from the dust has made you,
        Who savors you,
    Who knows you by name
    and now comes to reclaim.

For your Champion shall raise you
    with Pardon's full measure.
Earth's delight will one day rise up
    to embrace the treasure
    of God's steadfast love,
        now and ever.

∽ Inspired by Ps 103 ∽

Reverent ovation and wonder's avail

Bless the Lord, O my soul, and all
    that is within me, bless God's Holy Name.
Bless your Harbored Hope,
oh harrowed heart, and forget not
    the Anchor of your mooring.

The One who formed you has not forsaken;
    your failures no longer define.
As far as the east lies from the west,
    farther still shall our sins be removed.

The bridge of grace,
    unhinged by rage,
        will be restored.

Now parched with fear, your withered throat
    shall be quenched with a torrent of goodness.
Your fractured limbs and frail bodies
    are destined for healing relief.
Vindication is coming, you victims of torture!
The blaze of Heaven marks the way to mercy.

The One we adore is mercy-full and gracious,
    slow to anger and confounding with love.
God will not always accuse nor foment in anger.
God has no score to settle, no payback to unleash.

Like a father rejoicing in wombish disclosure,
    like a mother's delight
    in her newborn's first wail,
So your Maker exults in each heart's full exposure
    to reverent ovation and wonder's avail.

Inspired by Ps 103:1–14

Let gladness swell your heart

Listen, all you who stagger in desert waste,
disgraced by gloom's unremitting groan, dragged
daily to death's gate and the sea's drowning flood.

The Blessed One stands at the gate of plenty.
The Beloved waits by the well of refreshment.

Abandon your beggarly quest for breath beyond
the pale of praise, for sustenance beyond the tie
that binds all hearts as one.

Behold, every princely posture, every royal
presumption will heave and smash against the
shoal of Heaven's conspiracy with hope's insurgence.

On that glad day every voice of distress will confess
that sorrow's sway shall be displaced by joy's arousal
and resurrection's pledge.

∼ Inspired by Ps 107 ∼

By Thy might

Hasten now, all you whose life is spent with sorrow,
you of bone-wasting days, of sighing weeks and
storm-tossed years,

You who endure contentious tongues, threatened
by gangsters and banksters of every sort,

Come to the Sheltering Presence of the One who knows,

The One
    who tapes
        your photo to
Heaven's refrigerator door,

The One who rekindles in you
the gift of love on the wings of a dove.

～ Inspired by Ps 31 ～

Love of Christ

Sisters & Brothers, the Love of Christ is not
      an argument to overwhelm with the force of logic.

The Love of Christ is not manifest in gaudy acts of piety
      or opulent rites of purity.

The Love of Christ is not an authority to be upheld by
      institutional domain or bloody sword's advance.

The Love of Christ is not a bartered transaction,
      as if our plaintive promise to "be good"
      can unlock Providential attention.

Rather, the Love of Christ is an invitation to live
      according to a different rhythm.

By the Love of Christ, Siloam's pool washes
      muddied eyes to see the world afresh.

By the Love of Christ, every life-born-blind
      is claimed by grace in-fleshed.

By the Love of Christ, every fainting heart
      is freed for bold amend.

By the Love of Christ are feet secured,
      though the earth now heave and rend.

The Love of Christ is that embrace
      unlocking shame's reproach.

For the Love of Christ brings confidence
      in Mercy's sure approach.

∼ Inspired by John 9:1–17 ∼

Samaritan woman

Her name is never spoken. Only "woman . . . at the well."

In Samaria, of all places. Ancient Israel's redneck region,
    long ago decimated by Babylonian wrath.
Judeans of *proper etiquette* judge the land
    to be of suspect piety.

Trashy, whorish people
    (according to Jerusalem's devout).

Yes, Jesus knows. Knows all this and why you come to
the well in the noonday heat, rather than in the morning's
    cool breeze or dusk's dim relief.

O come to the well, in spirit and truth, for the cursed
    shall be first, every darkness a dawn.

O come to the well, in spirit and truth, for the cursed
    shall be first, every thirst be immersed.

Emptied of name and disfigured by shame,
    passed among men. (Whether by mortality's
        claim or idle disdain, we don't know.)
            But Jesus knows.

O come to the well, in spirit and truth,
    the abused no longer used
        or expendable or devoured.

And you know, as well,
    by the well,
        that all shall be well
            in the age yet to come.

~ Inspired by John 4 ~

Let the lost rejoice

When power reaps death from countless
killing fields, and every war sows the seeds
    of the next, those in the Great Shepherd's
        flock resist the bloodletting lure.

Let the mournful rejoice in the Lamb who
    rules, for the Tendering Day draws near!
Both lion and lamb are inheritors of the
    coming peaceful kingdom, but
        the latter's sleep is the sweeter.

Let the lost rejoice in the Lamb who rules,
    for the Tendering Day draws near!
When the grumbling accountants of shame
    and chagrin trap the erring,
        consigned to regret,

When the safeguarding coins are scattered, astray,
    and tattered hearts freeze with fear and dismay,

Let the ruined rejoice in the Lamb who rules,
    for the Tendering Day draws near!
How sure the delight of Mercy's pure light
    conqu'ring darkness and danger with cheer.

You who languish, forlorn,
    shall in pardon be borne by the
        ransom of Jubilee's year!

Inspired by Luke 15:1–10

Celebrant of mercy

From the Beginning, the Sovereign's harness of the seer's
    tongue assures a turbulent course. Announcing the
        surety of Providence among scarce-minded
        people—that's no way to cover a mortgage.

    Blessed is the tongue that proclaims God's ciphering.

To where may we turn for food that does not spoil,
for water that does not spill, for the bounty which neither
    rusts nor rots, unthreatened by thieves of every kind?

    Blessed are the hands of those who set
    the Beloved's table, bidding the least,
    the lost, and the lame to gather round!

As Wisdom sets her table along the parade of confusion,
    as Jesus lifts bread on the evening of betrayal, the
    called-of-God face contempt and endure dismissal.

    Blessed are the eyes who sing the song of Salvation;
    blessed, the ears tuned to the melody of God's future!

Fear not, oh celebrant of Mercy,
        God's slow-food Movement is underway.
The Table of Memory is set against the
    world's fast-food habits that fatten
            arteries and ravage hearts.

Therefore let us eat in plenty, cups overflowing provide,
    may this table's delight inspire earth's urgent petition:
        that one day, all shall eat and be satisfied.

Written to celebrate the anniversary of a friend's ordination.

III Transformation

By the Word of Truth

By the Word of Truth we are nursed and nestled.
We are cradled, caressed, and sanctified.

But the Word of Truth is more than flapping
tongue, more than motoring mouth, more than
syllable after endless sentence designed to
deceive and disguise and delude.

Not just comfort of soul does the Truth convey:
It embeds the mandate of earth's redemption.
All who are bound by liberty's law are pledged to
        Insurrection's promise:
                its covenant with widows,
                its assurance to orphans,
                its welcome to *strangers and aliens*.

Until the tongue can substitute for legs, use your feet
to do the Truth and walk its Way.

    But know this:
Doing the Truth may raise blisters
on your feet, calluses on your hands,
        sweat running down
      from forehead to finger.

Yet still, by the Word of Truth does
      the Beloved provoke.
May such Light dark's dominion eclipse.

∼ Inspired by Jas 1:17–27 ∼

Riff on Isaiah five-eight

"I'm really tired of your smells and bells
        and frills and thrills."
From the hollow of the Most High thunders the
complaint of Heaven against every piety peddler.

"Tired of your sanctimonious pomp and long-winded
        prayers; tired of your self-serving petitions
            for a downtown parking space."

Good God a'Mighty, when we say our *hail marys,*
        our *thank-you-jesuses* and our *god-bless-americas*—
            why don't you tip your hat and offer a prize?!

"Your prayer breakfasts don't cut it, given the way you
        treat school teachers and ICE-hounded immigrants."

You really want to galvanize Good-God attention? You
really want the Vindicator's might to dispel every blight,
every menace and every fret, every poacher, every threat?

Here's a hint: Undo your oppressive laws, and give the
        sinned-against a break.

Share your meal-ticketed fortune with the beggar-bowled;
        unlock the doors of warm houses for the frostbitten.

God just might bless such an America, and light might
        break through from your darkest cell blocks.

Maybe then your decayed cities will be rebuilt;
        your *makers* and *takers* find a common future.
            E pluribus unum, y'all.

∼ *Inspired by Isa 58* ∼

ICE – acronym for Immigration and Customs Enforcement, U.S. federal government.

This canyon of bleached bones

The troubling breath of the
Blessed One broke into speech:
"Oh human one, hear my question and answer rightly.
Can these bones *live*? Can *these* bones live?"

Only *You* know. Only You *know*.

"Then prophesy to these skeletal remains."

Oh dry bones, hear the Word of the
One whose breath brings refreshment.
Flesh shall follow sinew; moist skin
will be stretched in supple layers.

Breathe, oh dry bones, breathe again!
The rumble of life shall overwhelm
    the rattle of death.
Graveyards shall open and spill
    their captives into fertile fields.

Breathe, oh dry bones, breathe again!
    Fill your lungs with Spirit's Wind.
Sons and daughters, old ones and young,
    meadow and mountain, beast and bird,
the One present at creation shall be honored again.
On that day, no longer shall any govern
    by threat of the grave.
Spirit descend! Breathe on us, Breath of God.

Inspired by Ezek 37 & Acts 2

Getting in the way

Jesus said to his disciples:
> *Want to travel the Way with me?*
> *Then get over yourself, step out on the road,*
> *get in the way of every hostile host,*
> *and follow my lead.*

Gonna get on the Way, walkin' every day, no matter what they say or think, we're gettin' in the way.

Oh, but couldn't we just believe in you, Jesus? We've got lots of books on that, and bumper stickers to spare.

We're big fans.

Hop on the Way, walkin' every day, no matter what they say or think, we're gettin' in the way.

"We'll worship the hind legs off Jesus but never do a thing he says."*

Jump on the Way, walkin' every day, no matter what they say or think, we're gettin' in the way.

"We love to sing 'I have decided to follow Jesus,' but we don't bother looking to see which way he went."**

Set out on the Way, walkin' every day, no matter what they say or think, we're gettin' in the way.

Inspired by Luke 9:18–27

*Clarence Jordan, quoted in Dallas Lee, The Cotton Patch Evidence (New York: Harper & Row, 1971), 45.
**Frank Stagg, quoted by Relma Hargus, Lectionary Note Lent4A http://allianceofbaptists.org/PCP/alliance_blog_detail/lenten-lectionary-note-lent-4a.

That friggin' Lexus

Listen close, God.
When we get together and sing
"Down By the Riverside," we mean it.

But outside this sanctuary,
the urge to study war jumps up again.
    We all want peace, but we can't seem
        to get what we want without war.

It's not so much al-Qaeda
    [or, insert name of current national enemy]
that bothers us. It's our neighbors, co-workers,
    family members, or that friggin' Lexus
        that just cut us off in traffic.

So burn this chorus in our memory.
    Keep humming it in our ears.

I ain't gonna study war no more. . . .
I really don't wanna / gonna study war no more. . . .

Sister Anna

Sister Anna. Last-named prophet of Holy Writ, more
    likely listed among household property and livestock.

When did your Temple-dwelling vocation begin?
    What sustained your twenty-four-seven vigil
        for all those years?

> *Anna, school us in the habits*
> *of vigilant perseverance.*

How did those old eyes of yours spot the incarnation of
    God's redemptive Promise cradled in the arms of a
    Galilean maiden?

> *Anna, ancient saint and elderly sister,*
> *teach us to pray with urgent patience.*

Was it a hint from Simeon's voice, or a ghostly shade
    over Joseph's face?

> *Anna, bolster our resistance*
> *to despair's resignation.*

Or did the Light leak from Mary's gaze?

> *Anna, let prophetic vision shield us*
> *from profit's endless allure.*

And vouchsafe us, we pray, for Redemption secure.

∼ Inspired by Luke 2:36–38 ∼

John the baptizer

Such a tame name for a man born to inhabit
        the wild side of Heaven's incursion into
        earth's contempt.

You startle children with your leather-girdled,
    camel-haired attire, hot breath calling the
    devout into Jordan's penitential wake.
Witness to the Spirit-dove's descent,
    confirming Elizabeth's praise and Mary's assent.

What brings you and
    your honey-smeared beard
        into such a barren land?

Wade in the water. Don't mind the mud.
    A certain drowning is required as Breath
        from above is delivered on the wings of a dove.

The baptizer's bargain is this:
    There's no getting right with God.
        There's only getting soaked.

∼ Inspired by Mark 1:4–11 ∼

Too big for their britches

Jesus told his disciples a parable about those who get too big for their britches.

Who could that be? Hope it's not me.

Two men stopped by the hospice chapel to pray. One was spiritual-but-not-religious (SNR). Big on centering prayer, sweat lodges, Taizé music and Tibetan prayer flags. On top of that, he's an activist, an act-of-conscience jailbird, recycles everything, vegetarian, drives a hybrid, ACLU member, makes his own granola.

Could be me, if you add green tea.

The other was a tea-partying born-again beer-bellied redneck. Looks forward to county fair food and Charlie Pride and Patsy Cline music. Says *you'uns* when speaking second person plural. Eats Wonder Bread and baloney sandwiches and chews Red Man. Never heard of Jon Stewart. Tears up singing the national anthem. Wants the *guv'ment* to keep its hands off his Medicare.

Might be me, if born under a (really) different star.

When the SNR saw the beer-belly walk in, he paused his quiet Ojibwe prayer chant and scowled under his breath, "Thank Goddess I don't have his cholesterol level!"

The Wonder Bread man, having just heard his babygirl's final breath, cried out, "He'p me, Lawdjesus!"

So now I ask:
Whose prayer do you think lit a fire in Heaven that day?

∼ Inspired by Luke 18:9–14 ∼

The meek shall inherit the earth

There are many images in Scripture which express Heaven's purpose, but none more concise than this phrase from Jesus, the one we herald as the pioneer and perfecter of our faith:

The meek shall inherit the earth.

The powers that rule—and sometimes overtake our own hearts—consider the Way of Jesus a foolish option:

The last shall be first, and the first will be last.

The Spirit now calls us to worship.
The worship of God involves a declaration of worth.
So let us declare again the things that are worthy:

> *You have heard it said,*
> *You shall love your neighbor and hate your enemies.*
> *But I say to you, love your enemies.*

Day by endless day the world insists that you are what you make; that your value equals what you earn; that your worth accumulates according to your ability to hoard. Day by endless day the world insists that only the strong will survive. But Jesus said:

Do not store up for yourselves treasures on earth.

Day by endless day the world insists that ultimate
    power flows through the barrel of a gun;
        that mercy impairs strength;
that policies of dominance will ensure a life of prosperity.

But we believe the meek shall inherit the earth;
    that the last shall be first;
        that the way to peace involves
the risk—yes, even this, beloveds—of loving enemies.

Inspired by Matt 5:5; Matt 20:16; Matt 5:44; Matt 6:19, 24

Morning by morning

Be gracious to me, Blessed One, for I am in distress.

My eyes are awash with grief; my bed swims in tears.

My bones bulge under the weight of unlived life.

Sighs crowd my heart and swell my tongue.

Jesus, weeping over Jerusalem.

> Weeping over this city.
> > Over these people.
> > Over this church.
> > Over my own anemic,
> > > knuckleheaded self.

Can you *hear* it? Can *you* hear it?

But the One who vindicates is near.

The Advocate's approach stymies fear.

Morning by morning the Beloved awakens me,

Tuning my ear to Heaven's harmony.

Morning by morning new mercies I see.*

*Line from "Great is Thy Faithfulness," Thomas Obediah Chisholm.

Easter's aftermath

Easter resurrection is never as assured
as the arrival of Easter bunnies.

Clothiers and chocolate-makers alike yearn
for the season no less than every cleric.

And yet, in my experience, the Spirit
rarely blows according to the calendar,
much less on demand.

We live with ears open, eyes peeled,
hands and feet nimble, ready for
jolting news and a dash to one tomb
or another.

And this, apparently, is the purpose
of wakeful attention during the transition
    from Good Friday's darkness
        to Sunday sunrise:
training in the art of vigilance,
as maidens with well-trimmed wicks.*

One empty tomb poses no threat
to present entanglements,
    any more than annual and
        specially-adorned sanctuary
crowds encroach on Easter morn.

It's Easter's aftermath
    resurrectus contagio,
        contagious resurrection
that threatens entombing empires
with breached sovereignty.

Easter's aftermath

    The Lamb Slain sings
    of tribulation annulled,
        of death undone,
            of Heaven reraveling the
    sinews of soil and soul.

    Humus and human alike,
    "the earth and all that dwell therein,"
        inherit the promise intoned
            on that first dawn.
    Breath on truculent waves:
                    be still, be still.
    Wind on Emmaen travelers:**
                     Fear not, fear not.

    ∼ **cf. Matt 25:1-13. **cf. Luke 24:13-32* ∼

Keep it real

Sisters and brothers, listen to these words:

Wake up each morning
    with your mind stayed on Jesus.
You'll have to work at it,
    'cause there's plenty of distractions.

Don't give in to pretentious piety or fake affection.
    Keep it real.
Don't compete for status, but challenge each other
    to stretch compassion's sway.

Look after the needs of those on the edge.
Go to great lengths to find friends among the friendless.
Practice resurrection every day, especially
    when it's inconvenient.

Don't wrestle pigs. It only makes them mad,
    and it gets you muddy.
Pull out every stop to live in harmony.

Remember this: though you'll never finish your work,
    that doesn't mean you can abandon it.
Above all, love from the center of who you are, that place
    that God made and called *good* at the very beginning.

Inspired by Rom 12:9–18

Pace yourself

Sisters and brothers, don't be fretful.
Don't chew your nails or gobble your food.

Pace yourself, on both gas pedal and heart rate,
    so you don't race to ruin.

Don't faint in despair when the gunslingers flourish.
Don't let fearmongering threats upset your soul.

Let the confidence of Heaven throttle your breathing and
    the breath of delight inspire all that you do.

Don't go gettin' all worked up when the hucksters and
the hypesters and the sub-prime shysters come out ahead.

God knows their boondoggles and bailouts
    are coming to an end.

Trust in the One whose justice can be trusted: the meek
are preparing for coheiring the earth.

Wait on the One whose way is sure mercy, paved with
justice and righteousness bright as noonday!

∽ Inspired by Ps 37 ∽

Faith without fanfare

There are, to be sure, moments of high drama in the
work of holy obedience:
> marches to be made,
> confrontations to be staged,
> dangers to be endured,
> corruption to be exposed,
> trips made to distant and unfamiliar places,
> maybe even jail cells to be filled.

On rare occasions, the whole world is watching.

Much more often, the storyline of faith is lived without
notoriety, is forged without fanfare:
> in familiar places,
> in small acts of courage against petty tyrants,
> with commonplace forbearance in the midst
> > of garden-variety stress.

Much more often:
> with family and friends and neighbors,
> in traffic lanes and grocery store lines,
> with tired children and anxious partners.

Even—*Can you believe this!*—even in church.
Even more often:
> > with yourself.

To be sure, dragons need to be slain. Much more often,
> > though,
> gardens need to be groomed.

Ordinary time rocks

Come mothers and shepherds,
    gardeners and menders.
Come fathers and healers,
       instructors, defenders.

Hear the cheer of angels for your
big, bold, even brassy acts of courage.
Don't back down from the chance to be
    audacious, bodacious,
        maybe even contentious.

Yet it is the tenacious on whom
the Beloved most depends.

Foster the habits of daily attention
and timely words to encourage.
God's in the details;
      the devil prefers abstraction.

An inch of fertile soil takes a
millennium to amass.
Plant a coastal redwood, and
fruit trees whose yield
   you will not live to taste.
            Small stuff matters.
   An ounce of care
      is worth a ton of theory.

Quotidian faithfulness
in life's persistent,
   unremarkable moments,
when no bands play,
   no cameras roll,
      no headlines appear.

Ordinary time rocks

This is the persevering labor which
    Redemption most employs.
            Ordinary time rocks.

*Written for the first Sunday of "Ordinary Time"
in the church's liturgical calendar.*

Life transfigured

It is good and proper to give thanks to God.
And to petition these gifts of the Spirit:
Generosity, the secret of wealth.
Reverence, the secret of risk.
Trust, the secret of fearlessness.
Pardon, the secret of power.
Obedience, the secret of freedom.
Laughter, the secret of longevity.
Rest, the secret of resolve.
Humility, the secret of wisdom.
Comfort, the secret of boldness.
Lament, the secret of hope.

Transfigure our lives, O Christ.
Beckon us to that day when
all shall linger 'neath their own vine
and fig tree, and none shall be afraid.
Safe, secure from all alarms.
Leaning on the everlasting arms.*

~ Inspired by Mic 4:3 ~

*Last two lines from the chorus of "What a Fellowship," Elisha A. Hoffman.

Bodies in gear

Thus sayeth the Spirit, through the Apostle's letter to the church in Rome:

I appeal to you, beloveds, by the tender intention of
    Heaven's Delight,
let your *spiritual* response put your bodies in gear.

I've had enough—thank you very much—of your
    groveling prayers,
your profit-minded flattery, and every pissy-pious
    haggling for divine favor.

I want flesh-and-blood in the bargain, not your
    sentimental fawning.

Put some skin in the game. Put your assets on the line.

Put your corpus in motion to the rhythm of Redemption.

The *Spirit of This Age* is happy for you to give your heart to Jesus—or be at One with the Divine Presence—just as long as He-She-It doesn't mess with your bank account.

But you are to live by the beat of the *Age to Come*—
    (which—*Wake up!*—even now is meddling
        with the-way-things-are.)

∽ Inspired by Rom 12:1–2 ∽

The new deuteronomist

History says, Don't hope on this side of the grave.
It is too much to ask from mere mortals such as us.
    Yet we say, *Noli timere.* Do not be afraid.

Hope is not beyond your reach. It is not in the highest
    region of Heaven, or out beyond the farthest sea.
Hope need not be the exclusive province of heroic figures.
    Noli timere. Do not be afraid.

Hope is in your mouth, ready to be savored; it is in your
heart, awaiting love's harness. *Noli timere. Noli timidus.*

Do not be afraid, brothers. Do not be timid, sisters.

The time will come when the longed-for tidal wave of
justice will rise up, when hope and history shall rhyme.*
    Noli timere. Do not be afraid.

So then, live toward that great sea-change on the far side
of revenge. Believe that a further shore is reachable from
    here.* *Noli timere. Noli timidus.*

Do not be afraid, mothers. Do not be timid, fathers.
Believe in miracles and cures and healing wells.
    Noli timere!

Behold, the Beloved summons Heaven and earth to
    witness our resolve: blessings and life in the face of
    curses and death. Choose life, and rejoice evermore.

    ∽ *Inspired by Deut 31* ∽

Deuteronomist: One who accounts history to elicit response in the hearer. Written on the eve of a U.S. Congressional debate over attacking Syria, with lines selected and adapted from Deut 31. ∽ **From Irish poet and playwright Seamus Heaney's play "The Cure at Troy: After Philoctetes by Sophocles." "Noli timere—fear not" were Heaney's final words to his wife before he died 30 August 2013.*

Would that you knew

Weep, oh my soul,
with tears painful and public:
when life abandons ardor for order;
when the demand for sober security

upstages the generative prospect of passion;
when the birthright of fertile charism
is bartered for a ration of bridled expedience.
The blessed struggle—¡Buena lucha!—is upon us.

The City of Promise
is bathed in the tears of the Beloved
    —would that you knew,
        would that you knew—
who cries not in indignation or threat

but in persevering confidence
that this season of coercion
will be exhausted from its taunting
of the One who knows no revenge.

For this donkey-mounted Messiah
rejects all messianic folly
with announcement of an Empire
subverting all imperial ambition.

∼ Inspired by Luke 19:41 ∼

Blistering hope
A stonemason's meditation on perseverance

When cutting capstone, carefully measured,
from a larger block with nothing but hammer
and chisel, you come to know the necessity
of blister-raising toil to achieve envisioned result.

No guarantees are to be had, of course. Sometimes,
despite calculated scoring, tracing a careful contour
across one edge, 'round to another, and another,
and yet another, with metered strokes and measured
aim (fingers are no match against the carom of sledge)
the rock stubbornly declares it own gnarly cleft.

Some fractures are costly; some rocks just don't
cooperate in the prestige of being mortared atop
crafted columns. (But even these—the jagged rubble
hidden behind hewn face—have their anonymous,
reinforcing roles.)

Nothing, I say *nothing*, is finally lost.

To my amazement, though, most such cuts conform
to the experience of the ancients who first discovered
the cause and effect of arm-aching labor in fashioning
ordered edges. Such disciplined patience!

It seems implausible: that soft tissue of human hands
could effect an accurate rending of molecules so dense
the phrase "hard as a rock" was invented. And it is
accomplished without traceable progress.

Blistering hope

The rock well disguises its stress. Dozens of strokes show
no more effect than the first, and the splitting swing is
an epiphany. In such work, memory is more important
than manifest sight. The stone's sheer beauty is the
only interim award; blisters, the only gauge of progress.

Nothing, I say *nothing*, is finally lost.

How much less plausible the promises of other ancients:
that one day—*How long? How long?*—the serene
meadow welcomes wolf and lamb together; the shamed
know jeer-displacing joy; the fires of mercy forge
amnesty from enmity. How long, 'til the Beloved's
intention for creation coheres, prompting hope and history
to align?

The implausible has been promised. But not apart from
covenant terms of disciplined patience, of sweaty, achy
perseverance in pounding away—strike after metered
strike, with pauses to relieve parched and breathless throat
—at apparently impenetrable prospects.

Insurrection against the implausible is underway in
countless but largely-hidden places.
One or more within your reach.
Can you handle blisters?
And, sometimes, gnarly clefts?

Nothing, I say *nothing*, is finally lost.

IV Praise & Thanksgiving

On saying thanks

Gratitude is surely among the precious few
truly-renewable energy sources available. The
hearts of both giver and receiver grow larger
in the process. Saying thanks, especially beyond
the demands of simple etiquette, is among the
most accessible violence-reduction strategies.

It is quite possible, of course, that expressing
gratitude simply masks the desire to get in line for
future favors. Or fends off the possibility that one
is now in debt to the donor. Or is simply a disguised
form of doing business, as in gratuities—*tips*—to
those who serve us.

"Free" market values have managed to commodify
the most noble form of human exchange.
Freedom language has morphed
into a cover for savagery.

> *If you only give for what you hope to
> get out of it, do you think that's charity?
> The stingiest of pawnbrokers does that.*

Genuine gratitude, on the other hand,
disentagles us from such compulsory
and stingy calculations. It stems
from the recognition that

> *all good and perfect gifts
> come from above,*

On saying thanks

    which is to say:
    Good gifts do not originate with us;
    nor are they subject to our schemed rationing.
    We are custodians, not customers.

    Giving thanks delivers us from the deadly habits
    of hoarding. It acknowledges that all living—
    whether breath or blood, water or spirit—
    must flow, must not be banked, to be enriched.

    Thus the appropriate response to
    graciousness is to be gracious. Just as
    surely as water runs downhill, so, too,
    is glad-hearted life oriented to the margins,
    in the direction of those who lack the
    capacity to reciprocate in kind.

    When such gratitude abounds, life remains
    fertile. When it does not, soil becomes
    dust, available to every passing wind,
    choking lung and lake and landscape.

    I have endured such winds as a
        West Texas child.
    They made my nose bleed.

    To give thanks is to live thanks.
    All living is rooted in giving.
    Such is the ecology of the Spirit.

    ∼ *Inspired by Luke 6:32, The Message; Jas 1:17* ∼

Breath of Heaven

O Breath of Heaven and Earth's Delight,
to your shelter we flee from enmity's fright.

Incline your ear to each whimpering voice
collapsed by the weight of earth-splitting fear.

O Rock of Ages, refuge of sages,
deflect every threat of sin-soaked rages.

Let not the work of Creation's good pleasure
be subject to plundering, pillaging measure.

From murderous scheme and unraveling seam
deliver from slavery to freedom's bright dream.

Speak pardon to injury; mercy to adversity;
entreat us and greet us with grace-filled audacity.

'Twas your hand that caught us, squalling glee
with our lungs when, from mother's full womb,
we emerged: Praise be sung!

Unbind us, remind us, entwined as we are with joy,
adoration, dark night's guiding star.

∼ Inspired by Ps 71 ∼

The work of praise
Portending peace for the earth

The Blessed One does not stand in need of our praise; nor sits impatiently, impudently, awaiting our genuflection; nor strides restively, demandingly, threateningly, toward our cowering pose.

No, none of this. There is no protection to be warranted by proper groveling, calculated flattery, sustained applause, pleading curtsies or bargaining bows.

It is, rather, we who need to praise. By it we transcend self-serving ways. By it beggarly egos loosen their grip; anxious trembling and toil, stilled and rested; fury, calmed; moans, soothed; regrets, unknotted.

The Holy One of Heaven doesn't do booster clubs or sign autographs or make grand entrances at charity balls—or acknowledge the sky-pointed, victory-claiming index fingers of star athletes at moments of triumph.

God is not Number One. God is not an integer. God can no more be counted than the eye can see its optic nerve.

It is by ebullient praise that we become transparent. By it we send our presumptuousness packing. From it we readily marshal every asset and place them under the command of Another—Another, we discover, who is not alien to us, is not other-than, but is in us, through us, above, under and around us, who is with us as breath-to-lungs, blood-to-heart.

The work of praise

What feels at first like submission, we come to recognize, finally, as being at home, where we are welcomed and prized progeny to be feted, feasted, and royally attired.

In that union all that was broken is mended, all that was stained is cleansed, all that was doubted rests confident, all that was downhearted finds its hallelujah. We become as lovers to the Beloved. The weighty worries that previously occupied us, even terrorized us, are disclosed as so much falderal.

Personally, praise is like Pilates for the soul, countering the constriction of tendons and rusty joints, allowing freedom of movement and off-road adventures.

Publicly, praise is prelude to undoing every slaver's chain, every gallow's threat, every monopoly's reign.

The work of praise in the tent of meeting—*worship*, where questions of *worth* are determined and competing claims of *power* decided—begins in the labor of lament.

How long, O Lord (the psalmist's persistent introit), *will soul and soil be anguished and troubled? the wicked prosper? injustice stalk its prey?!*

Glory to God, announced the angels, *and on earth, peace*. Mother Mary then magnified the Lord for scattering the proud and lifting the lowly.

All praise is due to Allah, says the ancient crier (peace and blessings be upon him), *who delivered us from the unjust people*.

Praise to Heaven portending peace for the earth.

The work of praise

Praise is equally personal and public. It grows rote and rank when privatized for self-stimulation or adherence to pious rigor. It grows toxic when utilized as a tool for social coherence. Fully-blossomed, it loses all instrumental intent and rises "as in yonder valley the myrtle breathes its fragrance into space."*

The work of praise is both promise and provocation. By it we are simultaneously lifted to the ecstasy of beatific vision and launched into a world which fears doxology above all else.

Sing praise, all ye people.
Clap your hands, ye meadows,
    mountains, forests and fountains.
Magnify, ye birds and bees,
    creatures of seas, every lion and lamb—
        even you, Uncle Sam.

*Phrase from Kahlil Gibran, "On Giving," *The Prophet* (Oxford, England: Oneworld Publication, 1932), 19–20.

With courage impart

The Radiance of Day is my light and salvation.
No threat can entrap me, no terror encroach.

The Sovereign's my full-armored haven, safe harbor.
No storm can o'erwhelm me, no gale can prevail.

Though foes clamor 'round, bitter fright falls in torrents,
thy Sheltering Hand's dense defense doth surround me.

Cast me not, Gentle Savior, into grief's ruin and ravage;
for thy countenance only, I aspire and desire.

O Beauteous One, with rainbow adorned, insurrection,
resurrection, pure affection thy attire.

With relished delight all attest this confession: The
 goodness of God brims the land of the living.

I dare lift my head 'bove the raucous assemblage;
with joy serenading, Thy praises resound!

Be strong, oh my heart, with courage impart; neither leave
nor depart 'til by Mercy embraced.

Inspired by Ps 27

Weeping may linger

Discard your reluctance, you saints and you sinners:
Shout vowels of praise, sing consonants of delight.

On you, Dear Beloved, have I cast my care and
entrusted my fare. Let none rejoice over my sorrow;
let none reprise my grief.

In folly I abandoned the bonds of your Providence;
fool-hearted, my feet wandered wayward astray.

Take my mourning heart and teach it to dance;
tailor my grieving gown into festival attire!

O Radiant Refrain filling lungs with acclaim,
by your Name rid the earth of rancorous disdain.

Weeping may linger, the night's fright encroach;
yet daybreak reports hint of joy's sure approach.

~ Inspired by Ps 30 ~

Widow woman

The great and mighty judge had no use for God,
neither for people, save the few with favors to grant or
flattery to display.

Widow woman, widow woman,
    face bathed in tears.

Least of the judge's concerns were the pitiful pleas
of those with no standing in the courtrooms of the mighty.

Widow woman, widow woman,
    choking back her fears.

Confound this pesky woman!
Grant her justice just to shut her up!

Widow woman, widow woman,
    you done worn that ol' judge out.

Will not the Judge of judges hear?
Hear and respond? Respond and redeem?
Will persevering faith be found on the earth?

Widow woman, widow woman,
    time to sing and shout!

Inspired by Luke 18:1–8

Sip of joy

Beloved, we give thanks:
For those who plow and plant,
those who harvest
and those who harbor
the promise of the day when
all shall eat and be satisfied.

We give thanks:
For the day when all go out in joy
and are led back in peace,
the hills bursting in song, the trees in applause.

On that day no backs
shall bend in stress,
no arms ache or hands callous,
nor shirts drench in sweat,
with the bounty bound for the tables
of those whose eyes already swell out in fatness.

May that day mark the end of those
with no ears for the tears of distress,
with no pity on the forlorn,
scorning desolated souls
who cower and genuflect
in hopes of a morsel of bread
and a sip of joy.

∼ Inspired by Ps 73:7 & Isa 55:12 ∼

The ministry of encouragement

Encouragement is the lime and silica that cement fickle sand into concrete resolve. The ministry of encouragement is not the "soft," interpersonal side of our more hard-charging, public mission of confronting disruptive power.

> *We rejoice in the Blessed One,*
> *who draws us up and circles us round*
> *and builds a bulwark against gales of destruction.*

Offering pastoral encouragement within the Body is not "feminine" work where mission in the larger world is "masculine."

> *As the Scripture enjoins, weep with those who weep;*
> *rejoice with those who rejoice; and thereby reweave*
> *the unraveling fabric of the Beloved Community.*

Nor are habits of complimenting each other to be shaped by the logic of commercial transactions: I offer winsome words to you, anticipating you will return the favor, and more, later on.

> *O God who ventures into the pit*
> *of every human catastrophe,*
> *your ears catch the pitch of our cries*
> *which no mortal can hear.*

The work of encouragement is done to boost the soul's immune system. Encouragement does more than make someone "feel better." It's how we prepare for struggle.

The ministry of encouragement

> *Incite one another to love and good works,*
> *says the Apostle.*

Encouragement is the capacity to confront fatigue, failure, even desperation, with the confidence that God is not yet done. And neither are we.

> *Provoke one another to fidelity amid*
> *the world's faithless affairs. By so doing, the*
> *Evil One's power to rend us asunder comes undone.*

The giving and receiving of timely encouragement in seasons of severity opens a portal to Heaven's purpose and promise and power.

> ¿Es una buena lucha? Is the struggle a good one?

> ¡Es una buena lucha! It is good indeed!

∼ *Inspired by Ps 30; Heb 10:24; Rom 12:5* ∼

When you call I will answer

All who dwell in the dell of the Blessed Embrace
shall raise anthems of joy and grace.

My fortress, my shield, by mercy concealed:
O Shelter, my shiv'ring displace.

The Protector uncovers the snare of the fowler and
snatches from ravaging claws. 'Neath Redemption's
wide wings every heart soars and sings, every voice,
every hand, shouts applause!

The terrors of night shall stalk you no longer, nor the
arrows that fly by day. The pestilent shadows no longer
encroach, nor savaging tremors dismay.

Scuttle the fear of wrath's pure fright, all restive disquiet
allay. Confound the vandal of wreckage and ruin, and the
prowler lurking its prey.

With the Lord your refuge and holy abode, no evil
can track your ascent. Angels hover o'er you, their hands
to restore you, when feet stumble hard in lament.

"When you call I will answer,"
    says Love Everlasting.
"Cleave to me and none shall assail."

Now may honor adorn you, long life befriend you,
arrayed in redemption, your future prevail.

Inspired by Ps 91

Big band or bluegrass

Open your mouths, O people of praise.
Unchain your lungs and unleash your lips.

Let joyful noise erupt from every muted tongue,
thankful hymns from every muffled mouth.

Compose a new song for the Chorister of Heaven.
A cappella or symphonic, let the sound rise like leaven.

Whether big band or bluegrass or rhythm and blues.

Polka or hip-hop, bebop or swing. Salsa, Gregorian
or adagio for strings.

Waltz, mariachi, gospel or zydeco. Hillbilly, honky tonk,
ragtime or calypso.

Classical, Dixieland, sacred harp or sonata. Motown,
madrigal, tango or cantata.

Let the sea roar its tune, you harbors reply; you floods
clap your hands, you hills cast your cry.

The melody of justice, the harmony of grace,
returns for an encore of righteous embrace.

Regardless your rhythm, whatever your rhyme,
may the anthem of mercy keep you tuned and in time.

Inspired by Ps 98

Holy Great Smokies

Call to Worship
Come to the place where horizons expand, and the gulf
between earth and sky shrinks. Here covenants unfold
and confrontations are staged.

It was at Mount Ararat that Noah's ark rested on dry ground
as flood waters receded. From Egyptian bondage, the
Hebrews came to Mount Sinai where their adoption by God
was sealed and commandments were set.

> On Mount Carmel the prophet Elijah confronted
> > the false prophets of Baal.
> At Mount Gerizim and Mount Ebal Joshua instructed
> > the people in the Law of Moses.
> At Mount Nebo God brought water out of the rock
> > to relieve the people's thirst.
> It was on Mount Zion that David constructed the
> > temple as the center of praise and worship.
> Jesus' Sermon on the Mount outlined the vision
> > for the new people of God.
> It was on the Mount of Olives that Jesus prayed
> > through the night before his crucifixion on
> > > a hill named Golgotha.

Blessed by the Lord come the choice gifts of Heaven,
with the finest produce of the ancient mountains,
and the favor of the One who sprinkles dew on Hermon
and nestles among the pines on Tabor.

Your righteousness o'ershadows the Rockies,
your justice towers over Katahdin. Peak calls to peak
in your Wake and echoes back again.

Holy Great Smokies

Great are you, O God, and greatly to be praised.
Your holy Great Smokies are the joy of all the earth.
Break forth in singing, you Sierra Madres, you forests and every wild flower. For the Blessed One unveils you.

Blow the trumpet on every Appalachian ridge; sound the alarm on Mount Rainier! Let all the inhabitants of the land tremble, for the day of the Lord is coming.

In the abundance of your trade, says our God, you were filled with violence, and you sinned; so I cast you as a profane thing from my beloved Cumberlands.

Like blackness spread upon the Peabody Coal's sheared mountain tops, a great and powerful army comes. Fire devours in their wake, and behind them a flame burns.

Before them the land is like the Garden of Eden, but after them, a desolate wilderness.

Come, let us go up to Grandfather Mountain. There the Beloved will teach us the ways of righteousness that we may walk on the path of mercy.

Assurance of pardon:
    We cry aloud to you, O Lord.
    Answer us from your Olympic Mountains.
    Send out your Light and your Truth;
        bring us to your dwelling in the Wichitas.

Whoever takes refuge in God shall possess the land and inherit God's awesome Ozarks.

For you shall go out in joy, and be led back in peace;
the Bitterroots and the Black Hills shall burst into song,
and all the trees on Stone Mountain shall clap their hands.

On that day you shall not be put to shame and you shall no longer be haughty in God's blessed Berkshires.

Holy Great Smokies

Benediction:
In days to come the mountain of the Lord's house shall be established higher than Dinali; all the nations shall stream to its crags.

The Allegheny Mountains skipped like rams, and the Grand Tetons, like lambs. May the Adirondacks yield prosperity for the people; and the Davis Mountains, thy graciousness.

They will not hurt or destroy on my holy mountain; for the earth will be full of the knowledge of the Lord as the waters cover the sea.

On the Sangre de Cristos the Lord of hosts will make for all peoples a ballroom feast, a warehouse of well-aged wines. God will move among West Virginia's blast-scarred hills, removing rubble from each hollow and restoring every shattered-scattered crest.

The time is coming, says the Lord, when Matterhorn Peak shall drip sweet wine and the New Mexican mesas shall flow with it.

Death shall be swallowed up forever in the Kilauea's fiery depths. Then the Tender of Days will wipe away every tear, and all disgrace will be taken away.

∽ Inspired by Deut 33:12–16; Ps 36:6; Ps 48:1; Ps 133:3; Isa 44:23; Ezek 28:16; Joel 2:1–3; Mic 4:1-2; Ps 3:4–8; Ps 43:1–5; Isa 57:13; Isa 55:12; Zeph 3:11; Isa 2:1–5; Ps 114:4; Ps 72:3; Isa 11:9; Isa 25:6–8; Amos 9:13 ∽

In many ancient cultures, mountains were sacred places. Scripture's story of the ancient Hebrew people is punctuated with holy encounters upon mountains. This liturgy was written for worship following the arrest of a member of our congregation after his civil disobedience action protesting mountaintop removal coal mining in West Virginia.

Allahu Akbar

Let blessings leap from your lips, you People of Mercy!

For the One who saves is the One who serves.

Bring all that you are to this holy abode.
Take off your shoes and lean into God's breath.

Bring your heartaches and your hallelujahs; your
disconcerting fears and your delightful fiestas.

Bring your grinding disappointment and your grandest
dream; your seething sorrow and your side-splitting laughter.

Whatever you have, bring it here, lay it down.

For the One we adore is great beyond measure:
Allahu, Allahu, Allahu Akbar!

Clothed with majesty, the Blessed One lingers.
Awash in radiant light, God's chariot rides
the clouds, descending on winded wings, anchoring
the earth to its bedrock of hope.

Come joy, come sorrow, every day and every morrow,
every vict'ry and defeat now embraced at Mercy's Seat.
    Allahu, Allahu, Allahu Akbar!

~ *Inspired by Ps 104:1–8* ~

"Allahu Akbar" is an Arabic phrase commonly translated as "God is great."

V Songs

A Mighty Fortress is Our God

The challenge comes to everyone:
Disarm your hearts and follow
The journey Jesus hath begun
With joy displacing sorrow.
Be filled with mercy's might
To overcome death's fright
You warriors of the Light,
Assail earth's horrid night
The Resurrected One profess, proclaim!

Abide With Me

Open thy hand to every living thing
Hill, meadow, forest raise your voice and sing!
And in due season grant thy Jubilee
'Til then stir confidence, abide with me.

As empires rage, unbounded truth disdained
My soul grows weary, hope's approach restrained
When fears encroach and eyes no longer see
Blessed and Gracious One, abide with me.

All People That On Earth Do Dwell

All people that on earth do dwell,
Sing to our God with cheerful voice.
Let Resurrection joy foretell,
Life in the Spirit's breath rejoice.

The Most High One is God indeed,
Without our hand the world was made.
Yet would not leave us in our need,
But walks among us unafraid.

Therefore, lift hand in earnest praise,
With joyful heart rise up and sing.
Mercy now marking all our days,
Obedient love our offering.

Come, Spirit, set our lives afire,
With hopeful dreams of earth renewed.
With us abide, with us conspire,
For wrath's demise, all death subdued.

Nearer, my God, to Thee I cling,
May grace forever mark my way.
And though I face death's final sting,
I know Thy love shall ne'er betray.

Though darkness threaten Love's consent,
Though feet, confounded, lose their way,
Yet doth my heart rest, confident,
Of Incarnation's full display.

Amazing Grace

Oh happy day when hearts unfold
to grace and mercy's might
No more can mortal grief constrain
the realm of God's delight.

By pardon ruled, by praise renewed
Let every mouth confess
That Christ was raised and death subdued
To heal, redeem, and bless.

Come, Fount of every blessing tune
My heart to sing Thy grace.
Thy never-ceasing mercy streams
Prompt songs of loudest praise.

Last verse adapted from first verse of
"Come, Thou Fount of Every Blessing," by Robert Robinson

Beatitudes

Blessed are the poor, they shall all be raised
Blessed, you mournful, sorrow turning to praise
Blessed are the meek, all the earth be yours
Blessed, all the hungry-hearted shall endure.

Chorus: Rock on, you beatitudes, teach me to pray.
Rock on, you beatitudes, help me obey.
Jesus, lead me on along the Pilgrim Way.
Rock on, 'til the coming of the Bright New Day.

Blessed be the merciful, you'll get the same;
Blessed, pure in spirit, God will call you by name;
Blessed every peace-imparted soul, rejoice!
God-birthed children gonna raise their voice! *Chorus*

Blessed, when the persecutors wale on you;
Rejoice, be glad, God will pull you through.
Salt of the earth and Light for the world,
Good God a'mighty let your flag unfurl! *Chorus*

Sung to the tune of "Love is the Water," by Pat Wictor.

Breathe On Me, Breath of God

Breathe on me, Breath of God,
let gladness ring until
All things in heav'n and earth respond,
all fretful hearts grow still.

Breathe on me, Breath of God,
when threat'ning storms appear
Shelter me 'neath thy gentle wing,
banish all anxious fear.

Breathe on me, Breath of God,
hint of sweet rain, draw near.
Drench every soul, and soil alike,
awaken the seed of cheer.

Christ the Lord is Risen Today

Faith and hope—these things endure. *Alleluia*
Greater still is love most pure. *Alleluia*
Strong enough to face the cross. *Alleluia*
Death: no longer threat, nor loss. *Alleluia*

Who hath pow'r to ransom shame? *Alleluia*
None but Heaven's sweet refrain. *Alleluia*
Spirit come, cast out remorse. *Alleluia*
Pardoned now by mercy's voice. *Alleluia*

Mary, calm those frightened men. *Alleluia*
Peter, lift your eyes again. *Alleluia*
Magdalene, rejoice and praise! *Alleluia*
Paul, the Gospel standard raise. *Alleluia*

Come the Resurrection morn. *Alleluia*
Heav'n and earth renewed, reborn. *Alleluia*
Nations, hearts, alike disarmed. *Alleluia*
Lion and lamb lie near, unharmed. *Alleluia*

Doxology

O Blessed One, choired angels sing
Of life surrendered, offering
The power to bless as blessed we are,
To welcome strangers near and far.

O Ancient Promise, tune thine ear,
To pain and suff'ring, linger near.
Cast off the rule of wail and woe.
Thy tender love on us bestow.

O Jealous One, of cov'nant vow,
Recast the sword from threat to plow.

Remold Earth's fury by thy Word.
All flesh observe thy grace conferred.

May all my ways through all my days,
Befriend thy justice, sing thy praise.
Conformed no more to sin's distress.
Thy sovereign reign uphold and bless.

My heart's desire shall always be,
Nearer my God always to thee.
My soul, content, now finds its home
In sheltered hearth no more to roam.

These are the words we long to hear:
Sweet tidings sound, of hope and cheer.
Thus, in death's hour, our final test,
Our hearts secured, by love possessed.

For All the Saints

From earth's wide bounds, from ocean's farthest coast*
We praise the Name alone in which we boast
Seal our unity around Thy Host
Alleluia! Alleluia!

We stand amid the wonderment and woe
Caressing each other, as You our hearts console
Break forth in song, all creatures here below!
Alleluia! Alleluia!

Ringed by this cloud of witnesses divine
We feebly struggle, they in glory shine
Yet in your love our faithful lives entwine
Alleluia! Alleluia!

This mercy circle longs to shine your Light
Attend our yearning, restore to us our sight

By your grace our hearts with hope incite
Alleluia! Alleluia!

O love the Lord, with all your heart and mind
And welcome neighbors, make them kin and kind
Then to our Christ we'll ever be resigned
Alleluia! Alleluia!

Hasten the day, when tears no longer stain
All then shall rise to sing that great refrain!
Enliven our lungs to shout Hosanna's Reign!
Alleluia! Alleluia!

The saints are living still, their voices heard
Speaking, reminding, of Heaven's dream deferred
Hasten to hear, that earth's woe may be cured
Alleluia! Alleluia!

No greater love hath any than to yield
Privilege and pow'r to welcome and to shield
The least, the lost, the whole creation healed
Alleluia! Alleluia!

*First line from the traditional lyrics by William Walsham How.

God Be With You Till We Meet Again

God be with you till we meet again!
Mercy's claim to hold, endear you
Bread and cup to feed and cheer you
God be with you till we meet again!

God be with you till we meet again!
Grace unmeasured ever yield you
Spirit's flame protect and shield you
God be with you till we meet again!

God be with you till we meet again!
Let no enmity confound you
Hope be ever near, surround you
God be with you till we meet again!

How Can I Keep From Singing

Our Sovereign comes to make a way,
a path through raging water.
No enemy can reach me now,
for I am God's own daughter.
Remember not the things of old,
a new day is a'borning.
The desert sand shall bloom again,
all people's praise adorning.

Should ever death now cross my path,
I need not dread the morrow.
For I am loved, with breath or naught,
no longer bound by sorrow.
Though sallow days be mine to bear,
yet still the music's ringing
awakes my soul to hallowed joy.
How can I keep from singing?

Lead On, O King Eternal

Lead on, O gentle Pardon, though failures haunt our course
Let comfort and assurance, o'ershadow sin's remorse
Unleash your grace upon us, 'til hearts rise up, released
From barren hope and anguish, new life conspiring peace

Let All Mortal Flesh Keep Silent

Favor and affection contending
'Til the work of wrath confess
Steadfast love and faith embracing
Righteousness and peace caress
Magi wend their way to Advent star aligned
Dwelling place of God, earth-consigned

Wolf and lamb now linger, contented
Calf and lion peaceful arrayed
Cow and bear graze restful and fearless
Little child now marshaling parade
Roots from severed tree erupt, oh meek proclaim
Holy Mountain's knowledge and Name

Now the Day Is Over

Harbor not offenses, born of fearful heart
Sanctify each longing, Heaven's hope impart

Anxious toil confounding, fretful hands dismayed
Grant assuring presence, failing hope allayed

As the day, unfolding, love's incline renewed
Mark the Way, no more astray, enmity subdued

When eyes are finally shuttered, breath grown quiet and still
Angels lift and carry me 'cross the Jordan's chill

There no more my restless soul will burden'd be
Dancing shoes—just rhythm, no blues—laughter, joy and glee!

O Come, O Come, Emmanuel

O Come, thou fount of Mercy, come
And light the path of journey home
From Pharaoh's chains grant liberty
From Herod's rage, confirm thy guarantee
Rejoice! Rejoice! Emmanuel
Shall come to thee, O Israel!

O Come, thou Watchful Keeper, bestow
Glad heart, warm home to creatures below
Give cloud by day and fire by night
Guide feet in peace with Heaven's delight
Rejoice! Rejoice! Emmanuel
Shall come to thee, O Israel!

Secure the lamb, the wolf no longer preys
Secure the child, no fear displays
The vow of vengeance bound evermore
God's holy mountain safe and adored
Rejoice! Rejoice! Emmanuel
Shall come to thee, O Israel!

Arise, you fear-confounded, attest
With Insurrection's voice confess
Though death's confine and terror's darkest threat
Now govern earth's refrain . . . and yet
Rejoice! Rejoice! Emmanuel
Shall come to thee, O Israel!

Oh spring, from Jesse's root, the ransom flower
From Mary's womb, annunciating power
Bend low you hills, arise you prostrate plain
All flesh shall see, all lips join in refrain:
Rejoice! Rejoice! Emmanuel
Shall come to thee, O Israel!

O Come, announce the Blessed Manger's reach
All Herod-hearted, murd'rous plans impeach
Abolish every proud and cruel throne
Fill hungry hearts, guide every exile home.
Rejoice! Rejoice! Emmanuel
Shall come to thee, O Israel!

O Little Town of Bethlehem

O wounded town of Bethlehem
How sad we see thee cry
Above thy curfewed, empty streets
The belching tanks roll by

Yet from deep memory springeth
The hope of all the years
God's kingdom come
God's will be done
On earth, relieved of tears

Written in 2002 on the campus of Bethlehem University, Occupied West Bank, where our Christian Peacemaker Teams delegation took refuge (after being stopped by Israeli soldiers) while attempting to walk into Bethlehem during a curfew.

Precious Lord

When my trial draws near, and the judge appears
When the prison door is closed
Grant me strength to cling to Thy offering
Take my hand, precious Lord, lead me home

Written just prior to a church member's trial for an act of civil disobedience.

This Is My Song

O Truth Untamed, all boundaries bow before You
All borders bend according to your Word
O grant that every bitter heart be harbored
In sheltered cove, with Mercy's flag unfurled
Hearken and haste, Desire of every nation
Refresh the heart of hope too long deferred.

Let every mountain call to meadowed valley
And every stream, to ocean grand and wide
Let fertile ground announce the new creation
When all shall come, 'cross every great divide
O bell of liberty ring out for freedom
Break every slaver's chain, with hope confide

For all in Christ, there is a new creation
No more shall sorrow's cold embrace restrain
God's Rule and Reign unrav'ling pain with pardon
Transforming tears and fears to joy's refrain
Earth's host now reconciled to Heaven's harvest
The land, once tortured, bountiful again

Enlist all hands in reconciling measure
Ambassadors are we in Christ's domain
Attend your ears to this appeal, O Sisters
O Brothers, heed the reclamation's claim
A path now opens through the sea of trembling
From tortured cell, let freedom's way proclaim

Let peace be waged with courage and devotion
With warrior's brav'ry, vigilant and bold
Emancipation's melodies surround us
Each voice in harmony, all tongues enfold
Let Grace untold tame fear's unnerving sorrow
And sorrow's verse, to joy's refrain, unfold

~ Inspired by 2 Cor 5:16–21 ~

VI Occasional

Litany for Martin Luther King, Jr. Day

Admiring Martin Luther King Jr.'s dream is not the same as being captured by it. Too many respect the man but relinquish the mission, revere the dreamer but renege on the dream. So let us now recall the deep roots of that vision as spoken in ages past:

We remember when Hannah praised God by saying:
The bows of the mighty are broken,
but the feeble gird on strength.

We dream of the day when the wolf shall dwell
with the lamb. For the earth shall be full
of the knowledge of the Lord.

We long for the day when all shall eat in plenty
and be satisfied, and praise the name of the Lord.

We eagerly await the day when the lame shall be restored,
the outcast gathered, and the Blessed One will change
their shame into praise.

On that coming day, says Mother Mary,
God will pull down the mighty from their thrones
and exalt those of low degree.

Our hearts ache for the time when the People of God
will again be anointed with the power to
preach good news to the poor,
release to the captives,
recovering of sight to the blind,
to set at liberty those who are oppressed,
to proclaim the acceptable year of the Lord.

We still have a dream:

Litany for Martin Luther King, Jr. Day

    of a new Heaven and a new earth,
    when the Beloved will dry every tear
    and death itself will come undone.

    For we know that creation itself,
    now groaning in travail,
    will be set free from its bondage to decay.

    Ignite in us again the Word that stirs
    insurrection against every imperial reign,
    against every forecloser's claim,
    against every slaver's chain,
    until the Faith which death could not contain,
    the Hope which doubt could not constrain,
    and the Love which fear could not arraign
    lifts every voice to sing 'til earth and Heaven ring!

    Let our rejoicing rise,
    High as the list'ning skies,
    Let it resound loud as the rolling sea!

    ∾ Inspired by 1 Sam 2:1-8; Isa 11:3-9; Joel 2:19-26; Zeph 3:19; Luke 1:51-53; Luke 4:18-19; Rev 21:1-4; Rom 8:19-24 ∾

    Final stanza from "Life Every Voice and Sing" (also known as "The Negro National Anthem") by James Weldon Johnson.

The earth is the Lord's

At the conclusion of creation, God saw everything that was made, and behold, it was very good. Surely the earth is satisfied with the fruit of God's work.

God said: I will make for you a covenant on that day with the beasts of the field, the birds of the air; and I will abolish the bow, the sword, and war from the land.

Let the Heavens be glad, and let the earth rejoice; let the sea roar, and all that fills it; let the fields exult and all the trees sing for joy.

The mountains beheld the Beloved, and writhed; the deep bellowed and pummeled the air with its waves. The sun and moon stood still in their habitations.

Ask the animals, and they will tutor you; the birds of the air, and they will tell you; ask the plants of the earth, and they will teach you.

Praise the Almighty, sun and moon, praise God, all you shining stars! Praise the Lord from the earth, you sea monsters and all deeps, fire and hail, snow and frost, stormy wind fulfilling God's command!

Ever since the creation of the world, God's presence has been understood and seen in the things that have been made.

Jesus said, "If these my disciples were silent, the very stones would cry out."

Consider the lilies of the field, how they grow; they neither toil nor spin.

The earth is the Lord's

Creation itself waits with eager longing and will be set
free from its bondage to decay. And on the banks of
the river there will grow all kinds of trees for food. Their fruit
will be for food, their leaves for the healing of the nations.

∽ Inspired by Gen 1:31; Ps 104:13; Hos 2:18; Ps 96:11–12; Hab 3:10–11; Job 12:7–8, 10; Ps 148:3, 7–8; Rom 1:20; Matt 6:28; Rom 8:19, 21; Ezek 47:12; Rev 22:1–2 ∽

Written to celebrate Earth Day.

Poisoned sea, impoverished soul
A litany of lament over a despoiled ocean

In the beginning, darkness covered the face of the deep.

Then the Breath of Heaven swept across the waters, blessing the sea with all manner of creatures.

The sea knows its Maker and roars its applause; the fish therein leap at the sound of God's voice.

Through the baptismal waters of the Red Sea did the Israelites escape their tormentors and emerge to freedom's demand.

Surely, says the Prophet, the day will come when the whole earth will be covered with the knowledge of the Lord as the waters cover the sea.

Through the waters of obedience did Jesus enter the Way. By the Galilee Sea did he call disciples; on its waves did he come to them; by his power, its storm subdued. On its shore he revealed his resurrection insurrection.

But now, on our border, the sea has been poisoned. The deeps, made for praise, now drowning, voice hushed.

Poisoned sea, impoverished soul.
Hear now our plea; come, make us whole.

The oil of sweet gladness, the mark of rejoicing, now chokes the earth's womb, its legacy crushed.

Poisoned sea, impoverished soul.

Poisoned sea, impoverished soul

Hear now our plea; come, make us whole.

The fowl overhead, the fish down below, are fouled by the rupture of greed-driven lust.

Poisoned sea, impoverished soul.
Hear now our plea; come, make us whole.

Have mercy upon us, bring our hearts to repentance, and bind us again to your covenant trust.

Poisoned sea, impoverished soul.
Hear now our plea; come, make us whole.

Let us now pray for the ocean and the life it supports.

Written following the 2010 BP (British Petroleum) Deepwater Horizon oil spill in the Gulf of Mexico.

The octopus, too

Do you wish to inquire into the purpose
    of the Most High God?
Do you long for wisdom?

Do you pant for the breath of life?
Does the Song of Creation reach your ears?

If you ask the animals, they will teach you.
Ask the birds of the air, and they will tell you.

Ask the plants of the earth, and they will instruct you.
And the fish of the sea will declare to you.

In the Beloved's hand is the life of every living creature.

The day is coming, says the Beloved, when the wild
    animals will honor me:

The jackal and the macaw and the kangaroo.

The buffalo, the penguin, and the octopus, too!

~ Inspired Job 12:7–19 ~

Written for a "blessing of the animals" service.

All Saints' Day

The saints of old don't wear golden crowns, or sit on lofty perch, mouthing caustic comments on how poorly we yet-mortal souls measure up to the glory of days past.

They, too, knew about keeping hope alive while getting dinner on the table, faucets fixed, carpools covered, and budgets balanced.

After the ecstasy, there's always the laundry.*

The saints, too, endured wistful nights and wasted days. They had knees that ached in cold weather and sometimes spoke sharp words to dearly-beloveds—including, on occasion, to God.

You may never enter a lion's den, or travel through a war zone, or hear a prison door close behind your act of conscience. Mostly, you don't get to custom-design the witness you bear, the woe you endure, or the promises you make to mend the world as it crosses your path.

By and large, you weigh the choices that come your way without the fanfare of stardom's spotlight, your picture in the paper, or even angels whispering in your ear.

Saintly work is more common than you think.

---

*Line adapted from Jack Cornfield's book title,
After the Ecstasy, the Laundry.

Come home

All of you with voices, sing out! All who lack melodic tongue, raise the roof with joyful noise! If you have hands, clap them. Feet, tap them. Fingers, snap them.

Let even your eyelids blink out praise to the One whose delight drenches earth and every creature.

When you've had your fill of huckster dreams and foolish schemes; when exhausted by self-help gurus and stock market voodoos; when weight loss and hair gain on easy monthly payments disappoint:

Come home to the One who throws a party at your approach!

The Faithful One reclaims the breath of every death, adopting every orphaned child. Every martyr from every grave, every saint of every age, testify to Harvest plans from Heaven's bounteous stage.

Every storehouse now released, to all the lost and all the least, every belly, every beast, bless the Name beyond all guile.

You prisoner, take flight. You blind, give way to sight. Humiliation's reign, now stripped of fear and fright.

Every martyr, every grave, every saint of every age, gathers round to lend you Light through darkened days and restless night. Come home; come home.

Ye who are weary, come home.

Inspired by Ps 146

Final lines adapted from the refrain of "Softly and Tenderly," by Will L. Thompson.

Advent longing

O Wondrous One,
Who rides the skies
and consorts with the earth,
haunting the Heavens,
hounding mere mortals
with the expectation of ecstasy,
come and rouse hungry hearts
wandering this famined land
with the aroma of your presence.

Come, angelic envoys,
with renewed announcement
of glory *(to God)* and
peace *(for the earth)*.
Your people long for
Messiah's rejoinder,
through wombs made welcome
to the news of reversal:
the annulment of enmity
and the Advent of promise.

From Jesse's ancient stump
raise again a voice consonant
with hope's manger-laid disclosure,
of delight with wolf and lamb,
and children marshalling the
cavalcade astride the Lion of Judah.

O Majestic One,
whose passion spills
into flesh and blood,
set our hearts on the edge of our seats,

Advent longing

shivering in hope, longing,
longing for the age
when bitter memory
dissolves into magnificat.

As with our ancient sister Mary,
entreat us with the subversive promise
of Only Begotten freedom, begat
in the belly of holy submission.
May our lips echo
the jubilant manifesto
of creation's destiny
with justice and with joy.

Holy One of Heaven,
mark these dark nights
with the brilliance of your star
to guide emissaries of exclaiming grace:
of contradiction and scandal
to the insolent innkeepers of this age;
of blessing and bounty to the indigent,
to all who find no lasting home
save in the age to come.

∾ Inspired by the nativity stores of Matt 1–2, Luke 1–2, and lines from Isa 11 ∾

Boundary to benedictus
A meditation on Zechariah

Zechariah—
hillbilly priest of the
Abijarian house of Aaron,
himself the brother and mouthpiece
for "slow-tongued" Moses—
What lesion confounds your speech?

With Elizabeth—
cousin of Mary, spiritual heir of
Sarah, Rebekah, Rachel, and Hannah—
barren and bereft, seedless and sorrowful,
pledged to you, a priest of impotent prayer.
A union with no yield but malignant shame.
What boundary of belief constricts your credulity?

Afflicted with aphasia by Gabriel's reproach
'mid the cloud of incense.
The Holy of Holies,
designed to regulate the presence of
(the unspoken name of) YHWH, now
overwhelmed with dumbfounding Presence.

From your seed *(and Elizabeth's*
fallow soil) shall spring
    John—whose conception prompts
Judean astonishment: "What then will this child be?"

Speechless Zechariah,
befuddled cleric,
schooled in the theory of divine history
but unacquainted with its Advent.

Boundary to benedictus

For us, too, encountering the One
who promises the impossible
is a confusing, confounding prospect.
New life issues with a scream,
but is forged in the ordeal
of muted mouth.

Yet after a sojourn in the
wilderness of that bewilderment
even the silence gives way
to *benedictus,* to blessing.
The promise of perplexity
(for those up to the risk)
is praise and wombs leaping in joy.

Only by this unraveling
is the darkness dispelled,
is life re-raveled, is the boundary to
benedictus transgressed and the
tongue loosened for laudation.

    John—Naziritic preamble
to Mary's manifesto, whose very
name transcends ancestral boundary—
will reside in his own wilderness
until the time of harvest vocation:
        to turn
the hearts of parents to their children
        to give
light to those who sit in the shadow of death
        to guide
our feet to the way of peace.

~ *Inspired by Luke 1:5–24, 57–80* ~

Joseph

Obscured brother
consigned to the margins
of Incarnation narrative.
Carpentry-callused hands
now shield the shame
of sagging face, drooping, disgraced.
Chiseled lines prematurely sculpting
age in youthful countenance.
Thoughts of Mary smudge the heart
as tears smear the face.
Mary. Beloved. Betrothed. Betrayed?
Mary. With child. Whose? How, and why?
Joseph, companion in confusion
over God's intention.
No multi-colored coat for you as for
your scoundrel namesake of old.
But who dares answer, much less complain?

Joseph
Made redundant by the very breath of God.
What became of you?
Obedient to Heaven's outrageous instructions
amid Caesar's assessment.
Unable to provide more than squalid accommodation
in your beloved's night of travail.
Enduring embarrassed encounters
with wild-eyed shepherds and
strangely-clothed pilgrims
from obscure and distant lands,
each with incredulous stories of starry encounters.
Then hurtling toward Egypt—a land still haunted
by chained voices of ancestral slaves

Joseph

—only steps ahead of Herod's rage, the
Ramah-voice of Rachel weeping in the wind.

Joseph
Did compliance with Heaven's intrigue
cause your undoing?
Was it more than your pride could endure?
Or did Rome nail you to one of its trees,
anonymously, sharing the sentence
of countless other Palestinian fathers,
left hanging in imperial ambition
years before the similar fate
of Mary's fetal promise?
Did you map that road
for him as he did for us?

Joseph
Loving Mary more than posterity itself.
A future eclipsed by divine drama,
a fate unrecorded, left to the imagination
of bath-robed youngsters in seasonal pageants.
But not forgotten in the heart of God
or, even to this day, in the prayers
of shipwrecked sailors and
abandoned children.

St. Joseph
Consort of Mary,
accomplice of God.
Chaperone the prayers of all
who disappear from history.
Supporting cast in the
larger story of redemption,
leaving no trace other than the faint
moisture of tears on some beloved's face.
Vouchsafe the memory of such shadowed faces,
anonymous names, 'til their inscription in
the Lamb's Book of Life.

∼ Inspired by Matt 1:18–25 ∼

The manger's reach

O Blessed One, Beloved *Abba*, whose womb
squeezed forth all that is, humus and human alike,
animate and inanimate together,
sun and moon and galaxies without end.

O Sweet Deliverer, fruit of Mary's annunciation,
troubler of worlds and troubadour of Heaven's fidelity,
whose call to the table gathers the lame and binds
every shame with the promise of feast for the lost,
for the least, for the last, and all willing
to sing the angels' insurrectionary song.

O Wisdom of Days, breath of life in lungs of clay,
pregnant promise to Sarai and Abram, flaming
visage to Moses, whisperer to prophets and
confounder of priests. Answer to Hannah's lament
and Elizabeth's regret, tongue of fire on the
seer's lips and Pentecost morning's dazzling display.
Light from darkling sky that surrounds and
protects our way, even in death, sowing
Redemption's harvest with each martyr's blood.

Blessed be Your Name, that christening which
cannot be spoken or tamed but only proclaimed
in the risk of deliverance from the river of vengeance.

We gather at this portal of praise to lift our hands in
adoration: *Thank you. Thank you. Thank you,*
for the aroma of baking bread, the jubilance of wine,
the kindliness of friend and stranger and lover alike;
for the sufficiency of grace and the warrant
of ransom 'mid the wreckage of wrath.

The manger's reach

Yet we find ourselves, too, collapsed in the dust of
distress: *Help me. Help me. Help me,*
for the flesh we inhabit is shaken and shattered
by fearful threat and the agonized cries of
soil and soul who serve as fodder for the cannons
of discontent with your economy of *manna.*

As Isaiah foresaw: The envoys of peace weep
bitterly; the land mourns.* So now arise, as you
promised by the Prophet's scorched tongue,
and guide us to the safety and salvation for which
we long, earth and earthling in concert.

Make us rapturous lovers in this rupturing season.
Deepen the capacity for reverence, sufficient to
sustain the risk of Jordan's baptismal oath.
O Shepherd of fearless night, awaken in us the
assurance that one day, in the crumbling of empire,
mercy will trump vengeance—that one day, the
Manger's reach will exceed Herod's grasp and
every child shall rest fretless at your breast.

~ *Inspired by Isa 33* ~

Sorry, sorry, sorry

We kill and bomb
Murder and maim
Target and terrorize mostly
    (for high-tech armies)
from great distance
the better not to see actual faces
or severed limbs, or intestines oozing through
holes where belly buttons used to testify
to being a mother-born child

But then we apologize
    Sorry
        So sorry
            Deeply regret
                Such a tragedy!
                    Sorry, sorry, sorry

We do everything we can to limit civilian casualties
"This isn't Sunday school"
    (one politician's actual words)
Didn't have those children in our sights
Impossible to see, at 10,000 feet,
    whether Kalashnakovs are present
Smart bombs aren't flawless
Flawed intelligence
    (as if a test score were at stake)
Military necessity
Rules of engagement need refining
S**t happens
We gave them advance warning
War is hell

Sorry, sorry, sorry

The unintended consequences and inevitable
eventualities in hostile force-reduction and
counter-insurgency strategic operations
    (See "s**t happens")
Freedom isn't free
Do unto others before they do unto you
Asymmetrical warfare
    ("Why don't they come out and fight like men!")
No independent verification of claims of civilian massacre
    (aka, no one left standing)
"This is no My Lai" *(Vietnam, where as many as 504—*
    the Pentagon says only 347—unarmed women,
    children and old men were killed by U.S. troops, no
    weapons recovered, for which one soldier was
    convicted, spending 4 months in prison.)

We fight them there so we don't have to fight them here
    (which is why the U.S. needs 1,000 or so military
    bases outside its borders, dozens with golf courses)

Won't happen again, unless it does, then
                        Sorry, Sorry, Sorry
Video, and sentiments, at the top of the hour
    They left us no option
        Forced into this corner
             Them or us
                 Hearings to be convened
                     We'll get to the bottom of this
We need to wait 'til all the facts are in

But only eyes, no heads, will roll:
    foreign-born blood being cheap as it is
If war is the answer
    the question must be really stupid

Written after hearing one too many public officials rationalize
"collateral damage" against innocent victims of military strikes.

Limb by limb

Written for a worship service
focused on domestic violence

Men: Our hearts sag with sorrow when
the history of such misery is unveiled.

Women: Such truthfulness comes at a cost.
But worthy is the truth.

M: What good can come from such vile remembrance? Can we not safely and silently dispose of such memory?

W: No, not safely. Heaven still hears. The roots are deep. The seeds are dormant. The brutal harvest continues.

M: How then can we live with such terrible knowledge?

W: We can live because the truth unknots the cords of enmity. But first, a *NO* must be spoken with clarity, a renunciation must be made, before a *YES* can be asserted, before an affirmation can be announced.

M: Then let us proceed. Will you walk with us?

W: Yes, we will walk with you.

M: With the encouragement of you, our sisters, we renounce the habits of tyranny and intimidation. And we shall instruct our sons to also renounce.

W: With the encouragement of you, our brothers, we

Limb by limb

    renounce any silence and complicity. And we shall
    instruct our daughters to undertake such risky speech.

All: Breath of Providence, Breast of Provision, be near us
      in the midst of terror which assaults the bond between
      male and female, created in the image of Holy Intent.

Strengthen and sustain the ministry of Helpmate.*
        Fortify their voice.
Steel their courage in the face of resistance.
Enlarge their merciful embrace of all
        whose lives are battered and bruised and broken.

Beloved, bear witness to these promises.
        Confirm our repentance.
Grant bold resolve from hearts
        humbled by Your caress.
As we are endeared to You,
    so make us endearing to each other.
Limb by limb may the healing begin,
        in us according to your mercy.

∼ *Inspired by Judges 19* ∼

This chapter—accounting the torture and murder of an unnamed woman identified only as a concubine—is likely the most brutally violent narrative in the Bible.

*Helpmate is our local shelter for abused women and their children.

Building a culture of peace

As we enter this new millennium
we reaffirm our abiding conviction
> *that the God of Scripture manifests*
> *special concern for the cries of the poor:*

Of the marginalized, the outcast, indeed
all who have no access to the table.
> *We also believe that if the people*
> *of God are to be faithful to our calling*

We will locate ourselves in compassionate proximity
> *to those whose lives are battered, bruised and broken.*

We do so not as an ethical demand
or a work of righteousness
> *but as a spiritual discipline.*

For we believe that God's presence and voice
are most easily recognized and understood
> *in situations where life has been abandoned*

And hope is in retreat,
> *where death is on the prowl and despair rules.*

We testify to the Spirit's plea to
the church and to the world:
> *Disarm your hearts!*

Repent of your habits of violence and injustice;
> *return to the One who bore you in mercy.*

Building a culture of peace

Rebuild ruined neighborhoods;
    restore marginalized peoples.

Resume the politics of forgiveness
    and an economy of manna.*

Revive an ecological relationship with the created order,
    reject the escalating culture of violence,

and renew your commitment to
    building a culture of peace.

> *We lift our hearts to you, O Christ.*
> *Make us instruments of your peace.*

This poem excerpted from the January 2000 statement from the International Baptist Peace Conference in Melbourne, Australia, drafted by Kenneth Sehested.

*sufficiency

A Christian-Muslim call to worship

Of God's Unity, God says in the Holy Qur'an:
> Say: He is God, the One! God, the Self-Sufficient Besought of all! So invoke the Name of thy Lord and devote thyself to Him with a complete devotion.

Of the necessity of love for the neighbor, the Prophet Muhammad—*peace and blessings be upon him*—said:
> "None of you has faith until you love for your neighbor what you love for yourself."

Jesus said:
> "Hear, O Israel: the Lord our God, the Lord is One; you shall love the Lord your God with all your heart, and with all your soul, and with all your mind, and with all your strength."

> This is the first commandment.

The second is this:
> "You shall love your neighbor as yourself." There is no other commandment greater than these.

Say:
> O People of the Scripture! Come to a common word between us and you: that we shall worship none but God, and that we shall ascribe no partner unto Him, and that none of us shall take others for lords beside God.

The Messenger of God—*peace and blessings be upon him*—said:
> When God created the creation, he inscribed upon the Throne, "My Mercy overpowers my wrath."

A Christian-Muslim call to worship

To each among you:
> We have prescribed a Law and an Open Way. If Allah had so willed, He would have made you all one community, but [He wishes] to test you in that which He has given you, so compete with each other in good works.

As the Letter to the Hebrews admonishes:
> And let us consider how to provoke one another to love and good deeds.

The goal of you all is Allah; it is He that will show you
> the truth of the matters in which you dispute.

~ Texts quoted: Al-Ikhlas, 112:1–2; Al-Muzzammil, 73:8; Mark 12:29–31; Aal 'Imran 3:64; Sahih al-Bukhari 7404; The Qur'an, Surah Ma'idah, 48; Heb 10:24; The Qur'an, Surah Ma'idah, 48 ~

Written for worship featuring a sermon by a Muslim scholar.

Ordination invocation

O Wondrous One,
who rides the skies and
consorts with the earth,
who haunts the Heavens,
hounding mere mortals
with the expectation of ecstasy,
come and incite us to
Heaven's revolt against
earth's revenge.
Revive hungry hearts
wandering this arid land
with the aroma of your presence.

Fire of Heaven,
scorch away the encrusted
results of living so long
outside the breath of your lungs.
Rekindle your blaze
in the marrow of our souls.
As Jesus was raised
in Easter's Resurrection Moment,
now animate your people
on this Pentecost Sunday,
and breathe new life into your
Resurrection Movement.

O Majestic One,
whose passion spills into flesh and blood,
bless the one who kneels in this assembly.
She is fruit of your womb,
anointed with your presence,
acknowledged by these witnesses

Ordination invocation

as an arsonist of the Spirit.
As with our ancient sister Mary,
draw forth from her lips
the subversive announcement of
Heaven's claim on earth's abandoned.

Bread of Heaven,
with our hands implant your
fingerprint on her forehead, sign
of contradiction and scandal
to the gods of this age,
of blessed bounty
for the age to come.
Make her voice strong,
her feet nimble.
May she ever revel as one
made in your image.
Give her death-defying courage,
holy rage and tender mercy.
Instill salty savor,
leavening wisdom,
and guiding light.

Written and then adapted for the ordination services of several friends.

Water of life: a baptismal prayer

We thank you, God, for water.
By it you give life to plants,
animals, and all humankind.

We thank you that in the beginning
your Spirit of creation moved over
the face of the waters.

We thank you for your rainbow
covenant promise that emerged from
the drowning floodwaters.

We thank you for safe passage
of our ancestors through the Red Sea,
from slavery to freedom.

We thank you for quenching the
thirst of our forebears with water
from the rock at Horeb.

We thank you for the Heaven-parting,
dove-accompanying baptism of Jesus
in the River Jordan.

We thank you for Jesus,
who stilled raging water;
who offered living water,
a spring of water welling up
    to eternal life;
who washed the disciples' feet
to signify their continuing vocation.

Water of life: a baptismal prayer

We thank you, God, that you
have led us by still waters.

We thank you for the promise
that one day justice will flow like the waters,
righteousness like an everflowing stream.

We thank you for creating us
in the watery womb of our
mothers and for recreating us
in the watery womb of baptism.

   This is our confession:
Having been buried with Christ into death,
knowing that Christ was raised from the
dead by the glory of God,
we ourselves are raised to
walk in the newness of life.

Amen!

Co-written with Nancy Hastings Sehested.

Ten years

How well I remember standing there on the
Sidewalk in Santa Fe in front of a jewelry store
      where you'd just picked up your rings.

My wife of twenty-seven years, me, the two of you.
The two of you trying your best not to melt into the
      pavement under the weight of emotions;

The two of us with eyes watering from the
Holy smoke from some nearby burning bush,
      wondering if we should take off our shoes.

We went to a Lyle Lovett concert that night,
And as a concluding encore he sang that old
Gospel hymn, with its refrain,
      While on others thou art calling,
      do not pass me by. . . .*

And, sure enough, a cool breeze broke the heat and
Made us shiver. Such delight. Such pure delight,
      nestled within the sun-soaked faces

And scuffed boots of year after multiplied year
Of faithfully-attentive gaze and lovesome
      perseverance.

I stumble into grace just
      remembering.
Here's hoping the rains find your pastures.

Written to commemorate a decade of covenant ties (unrecognized by state authorities) with the purchase of rings.

*Line from "Pass Me Not, O Gentle Savior," Fanny Crosby.

Acquainted with grief

We are a people acquainted with grief.
In the bonds of this Body none need be embarrassed
    at the sound of sobbing, of the soul's aching groan.

Here the tear is neither
    uncommon nor unwelcomed.

Here the strong confess their doubts,
    the fluent run out of words.

Here the gentle speak their rant and
    the hesitant shout their rage.

Here we acknowledge life's daily
    bout matching
        faith with fear,
        hope with despair,
        love with contention,
        and joy with complaint.

We do so for matters whether
        small and personal,
        or large and public;
        whether near or afar,
        both named and anonymous.

Despite the odds-maker's wager,
    we march on unencumbered:
        Sustained by the cadence
            of enamoring grace.

How dare the sun ascend

We all knew it would come.
    Someday. Always later.
        Mañana.
It comes for us all. Sure.
        Of course.
    We know that. Someday.
        Mañana.

But when *someday* draws near
    for someone you love
        whose silenced breath sears
            your lungs with flames of grief
        and sobs so immense
    you wonder:
How dare the sun ascend?
    The stars to shine?
    Even the yeast to rise!

Who authorized the earth to turn another inch?
    Gravity itself should be suspended,
and the new moon halt in midair
    with its ghostly light exposing
        every predator's stare.

All words—every syllable—fail and flail about
    as if comfort answers to incantation,
        as if death leaves no bruise,
    as if sorrow can be *shhushhed* away like
        crows from the cornfield.

How dare the sun ascend

Only flesh on flesh can convey
    the pledge, to shivering hands and quivering hearts,
        the implausible news that dust is not the end.
Only cheek to cheek,
    and mingled tears,
        chase back fears
to their perditious haunt.

For the soul come undone,
        let skin speak to skin, with hands'
        gentle brace of countenance consumed
in doleful, woeful recoil.
The dirge will
    have its day,
        the sigh will have its say.
    But not more, not a minute
        more, than its allotted time.

For the day lies in wait
        when fear will be trumped,
    every tear sated, every
mournful lament yielding the floor
        to the sound of angels clogging,
            feet pounding parquet
in rhythmic cadence,
    whirling and twirling,
        with shouts of delight
and volleys of glee
    harmonized
        by fiddle and banjo and bass.

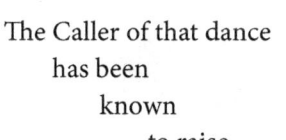

The Caller of that dance
    has been
        known
            to raise
                the dead.

In memorium and celebration of the life of a deep-souled friend.

The breadth of Heaven's reach

A life in Christ is
        an invitation
to live according to a different rhythm.

It stimulates the courage to
        move forward
even when the path seems to crumble
beneath our feet, when every way forward
            is shrouded in threat.

The Love of Christ is that embrace which
        untangles the anxious heart
        and calms the fretful hand
where fears are overruled by confidence and
        trembling is tempered
with pardon and permission.

It is the still, deep stream amid
every tempest that knows
        nothing, nothing,
can separate us from the
        length and breadth
            of Heaven's reach.

Written as a beloved's funeral benediction.

Let the banquet begin

O happy day when friends return from
afar, safe, unharmed, fingers, toes and
taste buds intact, hearts strong (though
weathered from the journey), long past
ready to put suitcases away, for more

walks in the woods and the familiar
faces of bloodkin and soulfriends.
Long past ready for snuggling with
familiar soil and hugging delicious
necks, belly-button to belly-button,

with time to relish memories of the
year now sprinted by. Good times
past, and sweet; hard times, too,
and some sour, and surely too
many miles, ever struggling to

understand and be understood, and
hot-sweaty times, clothes pasted to
skin but also with salt-scented
Caribbean breezes, all this, and more.
Not to mention having stood, time after

time, exposed to the breath of the Spirit.
And not the soft-gentle-sentimental kind,
more like the squall of a wind tunnel,
like jalapeño concentrate, like the
towering, lightning-filled cumulus sky

whose signature inscribes so many Cuban
late afternoons. Time to rest from such

Let the banquet begin

    rigor. The heart can take only so many
    leaps and adrenaline darts. Time to soak
    and saunter and ponder
        what it means
            to be nothing,
                yet everything,
                    at the same
                      time.

No doubt, there is a tearing in returning,
a certain severing of immediacy with mercy
on that far edge. But the seeds of your
learning were surely planted deep. Time
now to let them grow and blossom and

bear fruit to both nourish and delight
the rest of us—we who tracked your
movements from this distance, who
marked the calendar, whose faces lit up
when your names appeared in our email

in-boxes (knowing how much work was
required of you for each and every one)
—for we sense that you bear in your bodies
the compass readings toward a new horizon
by which we, too, can set our sights and

plot our journey. All that you have sought
and seen and savored—with provisions no
greater than the child at Jesus' impromptu
picnic—shall feed a multitude and to spare.
Let the banquet begin.

Celebrating the return of good friends after their year in Cuba.

VII Benedictus

Lean toward the land

Oh people of Promise, let your eyes arise to the
hills above the hollows, where a cleft is prepared
and your sustenance is proffered.

God will not let your foot be moved. Heaven's
Sheltering Wing neither sleeps nor slumbers.

The MercyFull One is your keeper. The tree
of righteousness towers above you.

Under its shading presence the sun shall not
harass you by day, nor the moon haunt you by night.

The Blessed One will keep you from all evil
and will sustain your life.

Therefore lean toward the land whose warrant
wills that all lament shall yield to laughter.

Let your hearts be upheld by the Presence
who lingers in love above your going out
and your coming in,

between your harbor safe and the sea's contention,
from this day on, from now and henceforth.

Forever and ever and ever, *Amen!*

~ *Inspired by Ps 121* ~

House of meeting

And now
and now
in this house of meeting
as daylight ends
and darkness descends
prepare your hearts for God's greeting

Though hearts ache by night
joyful blaze will ignite
with the radiance of Love
that will *not* let you go

Will *not* let you go
Will *not*
Will *not*
Will *not* let you go

Go out in joy

What is it you wish to know, oh mortal one?

Do you think you must ascend to the highest Heaven
or descend to the deepest pit?

Do you not know that Wisdom has pitched a tent in your midst?

Ask the four-legged, and they will mentor you, or the
winged-of-air, and they will school you;

Or speak to the earth, and it will teach you, or let the fish
of the sea inform you.

Who does not know that the Gracious Host has done this?

In the Blessed One's reach is the heart of every creature,
the breath of every living thing.

Brother Sun declares the Beloved's glory. His voice goes
out o'er all the earth, his words to every habited place.

Sister Moon and stars pour forth speech to brighten the
night in splendor and counsel.

Now hear the blessed promise of old, made new in your hearing:

May you go out in joy and be led back in peace,
the hills bursting in song, the trees in applause!

*Inspired by Job 12:7-10; Ps 19:1-4; Ps 97:6; Isa 55:12
and St. Francis of Assisi's "Canticle of the Sun."*

The last word: a wedding blessing

May you store up patience, for life is not always kind,
and you need to persevere.
    Remember that regret is not the last word.

Despite life's disregard, *the last word is this*:
        One day every cup will overflow.

May you store up affection, for sometimes the heart
grows cold, and you need to persevere.
    Remember that bitterness is not the last word.

Despite every cold-hearted season, *the last word is this*:
        One day the sun's warm embrace will thaw every
            brittle grimace.

May you store up mercy, for life is not always gentle,
and you need to persevere.
    Remember that enmity is not the last word.

Despite life's brutal stain, *the last word is this*:
        One day pardon will trump vengeance.

May you store up forgiveness, for life is not always charitable.
    Remember that judgment is not the last word.

Despite all cruel reproach, *the last word is this*:
        One day grace will have its way.

May you store up hope, for life is not always buoyant,
and you need to persevere.
    Remember that despair is not the last word.

The last word: a wedding blessing

Despite all dismay, *the last word is this*:
    One day the meek will inherit the earth.

May you store up faith, for life is not always devout,
and you need to persevere.
    Remember that infidelity is not the last word.

Despite life's treacherous grip, *the last word is this*:
    One day creation itself will shed its decay.

May you store up praise, for life is not always jubilant,
and you need to persevere.
    Remember that lament shall not have the last word.

Despite every mother's grief, every father's sorrow,
the last word is this:
    One day those who sow in tears will reap
        with shouts of joy.

∾ Inspired by Ps 23:5; Zeph 3:19; Rom 8:19–24; Ps 126:5 ∾

For that Bright Land

It's us, it's us, it's us, O Lord,
standing in the need of prayer.
It's our neighbor, it's our nation,
its creation that's groaning,
standing in the need of prayer.
     Groaning with sighs

too deep for words, singing our
woebegone songs for the world
that is promised from
     Beyond every prediction
     Beyond every market forecast
     Beyond every rule of engagement
     Beyond, at times, even our own faltering faith.

Sisters and brothers, why are we here, again,
week after bloody week,
     weak after so much weary,
          warring news?

It is for that Bright Land that we squint to see!

What if we woke up this morning
     with our minds stayed on freedom?
Stayed on freedom, about which
     politicians banter but secretly fear.

And what if we woke up this morning
     stayed on Jesus?
Stayed on Jesus, who moves among us,
     incognito, inviting, enticing,
        calling from the margins:
              Over here! Follow me!

Inspired by Rom 8:18–27

Blessings, benedictions & charges
Excerpted from sundry pastoral notes

The power to bless and the work of encouragement are likely the most commonly overlooked assets we possess— probably because the openings to do so are common and ordinary, lacking the theatrics by which we so often assess the Spirit's presence in the world.

§ § §

May you find treasures hidden in plain sight. Hear melody amid thunder. Trace mercy's work in the face of mayhem's constant threat.

§ § §

Never forget: We often sow for an unseen harvest; provide hospitality for angels unaware; set tables of bounty for unnumbered migrants to the land of Heaven's delight.

§ § §

Proclaim with confidence the Beloved's promise to those who live in the ashes: Thus says the Host of Heaven: "I will restore to you the years which the locusts have eaten." *(Joel 2:25)*

§ § §

May you fall in love with God without promise of paradise or threat of hell.

Blessings, benedictions & charges

§ § §

May you always be up to something good, inspired by something hopeful, drenched in something beautiful, embedded in something larger, made generous by something extravagant, and fired by the passion which one day will scour the world of its deadly infection.

§ § §

Never allow the enormity of the world's grief to paralyze you. Savor this teaching from the Talmud: "You are not obligated to complete the work, but neither are you free to abandon it." *(Pirkei Avot 2:21)*

§ § §

May the road rise up to meet you . . . just not square in the face.

§ § §

When the editors and the critics and the merely curious finish with you—whatever their conclusions—may they know they have wrangled with truthtellers.

§ § §

In every season of confusion, remember the adage: When no new Word from the Lord is heard today, continue living in fidelity to the one spoken yesterday.

§ § §

To a friend headed to a highly conflicted region. There will be times when you feel the urge to keep your head down, but you know to do so would cause you to miss important things. And then there are times when you *really do* need to keep your head down. Unfortunately, learning the difference between the two usually involves making mistakes as to which is which. Hopefully, none that are fatal, but there are no guarantees. Just trust that you will, in the end, receive what you most need.

§ § §

May your life ring true, its peal declaring pardon to the sound of every torment.

§ § §

Remember that your welfare is not tied to your sovereignty but to your contingency. It's not in your independence but in your interdependence. Not in your autonomy but in your interrelatedness. Not in your solitude but in your affiliation. Not in your self-sufficiency, but in your mutuality.

§ § §

May your dawns ever bring renewed curiosity, your dusks the pleasure of rest.

§ § §

Sometimes the "center" to which our centering prayer calls us is smack dab in the middle of the world's decentered, disoriented, disabled and dysfunctional life.

§ § §

Blessings as you, your family and friends trumpet your mother's lively memory, grieve her breathly absence, and serenade her crossing that great and joyous Threshold of Welcome to the Arms of Delight and Comfort.

Blessings, benedictions & charges

§ § §

May your dreams be bold. May you know a strong and gentle grace when you and others fail, never fearing to begin again—and again and again. Bow the knee to no one, save those occasions when the Center bids your fingers to dig for your life.

§ § §

To an ordination candidate. You have an extraordinary gift. And it really is a gift. Why some get it and others don't is mysterious, and you'll never get to the bottom of why this is so. Just remember: You don't own this gift. It is a gift to the whole damned-but-beloved world. Be careful with this gift. It's not a trophy. If you ever try to use it in a conceited way—no doubt you will be tempted to do so, since hubris is an equal-opportunity virus—it will bite you in the ass.

§ § §

May you live large, laugh often, and love well.

§ § §

Never forget that the One who draws us together, who mends our threadbare parts, is greater than the one who separates and segregates and tears at our seams.

§ § §

Remember, if you dare, the Jesus-named *Abba* is One whose movement often trespasses on religious authority, proper social standing, predictable economic forecasts, and political maneuvering of every sort. There is an *otherness*, a *wildness*, one could even say a *queerness* to this One which does not submit to ecclesiastical management, cultural propriety, futures market predictions, or congressional oversight.

§ § §

May you have each other always—and want to.*
May you know that in this wedding feast the Holy Spirit is establishing another beachhead in a fickle and faithless world. It is said that when Jesus rescued the wedding feast at Cana, turning common water into vintage wine, it was done to reveal the glory of God. Don't you like that—*vino for the glory of God!*

*Les Murray, Collected Poems (Victoria, Australia: Black Inc), 381.

§ § §

Keep on praising, because praise is our most potent form of protest. The practice of praise is the pedagogy of hope. Only those who know how to praise can confront the world's deep pain and not be overwhelmed.

§ § §

Tribulation is the normal circumstance for *stilled-ones* in a frenzied, fretful world whose currency is the power to exclude and dominate. Be still, be of good cheer, have courage, for that world is being dismantled *(cf. John 16:33)*.

§ § §

Your grief may be irresistible. Neither bless nor repress the ache that saturates every wakeful moment. Just turn to it and say: "I see you there, Mr. Boogeyman. Stay as long as you like, but here you'll get neither bed nor board!"

Blessings, benedictions & charges

§ § §

That's what grace does—it circulates, without proprietary claim by any, to all. It is so anti-capitalist, which is why, despite much pirating and cheap knock-offs, it is still such a scandal in a land governed by the rule of desert.

§ § §

May you know when to labor—fearlessly, relentlessly, urgently. And when to rest—indulgently, languidly, in Sabbath's playfulness.

§ § §

The future is beyond your ability to manufacture or engineer. To be sure, it will require your active participation, but it can only be noticed, and entered, on bended knee.

§ § §

Move on in the confidence that, should you be swallowed in some hidden crevasse, you'll discover it's only the fold of your Lover's arm.

§ § §

May you live to see the day when mercy trumps vengeance—the day when all that has been shamed and shackled and shattered will be restored to praise and doxology, according to the Promise which was, which is, and which ever shall be.

§ § §

In the end, all we can say about the results of our efforts is this: That we sensed the Spirit stirring, at particular times and places; and that we threw caution to the wind, adjusting our sails to catch that mighty Breath, willing to go wherever we were taken.

Scripture reference index

Some Scripture texts referenced are direct quotes or paraphrases. Most frequently, though, the text has "inspired" the work, often with the use of key words, phrases or insights.

Genesis
1:31	105–106

Exodus
13:17–22	8
17:6	20
20	13

Deuteronomy
8:1–10	7
31	62
33:12–16	83–85

Judges
19	122–123

Ruth
	20

1 Samuel
2:1–8	103–104

2 Kings
6:8–23	29

Job
12:7–8, 10	105–106
12:7–10	143
12:7–19	109

Psalms
3:4–8	83-85
17	23
19:1–4	143
23:5	144–145
27	75
27:13	xvii
30	76; 79–80
31	35
36:6	83–85
37	56
43:1–5	83–85
46	11
48:1	83–85
63	23
71	30; 71
72:3	83–85
73:7	78
91	23; 81
96:11–12	105–106
97:6	143
98	82
103	32
103:1–14	33
104:1–8	83–85
104:13	105–106
107	34
114:4	83–85
118	10
126:5	144–145
121	141
130	11; 27

Psalms (continued)

133:3	83–85
146	111
148:3, 7–8	105–106

Proverbs

29:18	21

Isaiah

2:1–5	83–85
11	112–113
11:3–9	103–104
11:9	83–85
25:6–8	83–85
30	123
33	118–119
44:23	83–85
45:15	6
55:12	78; 83–85; 143
57:13	83–85
58	44
61:1–2	5
66:22	xix

Jeremiah

1:4–10	30
15:16–19	15
29:1–14	16
31	28

Ezekiel

28:16	83–85
37	45
37:1–14	9
47:12	105–106

Hosea

2:18	105–106
11	12
14	23

Joel

2:1–3	83–85
2:19–26	103–104

2:25	147

Amos

9:13	83–85

Micah

4:1-2	83–85
4:3	60

Habakkuk

3:10–11	105–106

Zephaniah

3:11	83–85
3:19	103–104; 144–145

Zechariah

7:6-10	29

Matthew

1:18–25	116–117
1–2	112–113
4:1-4	29
4:1–11	7
5:5	51
5:44	51
6:19, 24	51
6:28	105–106
7:7–8	12
13:52	xi
20:16	51
25:1-13	53–54

Mark

1:4–11	49
5:1–20	17
12:29–31	126–127

Luke

1	23
1:5–24, 57–80	114–115
1:51-53	103–104
1–2	112–113

2:36–38	48
4:18	5
4:18–19	103–104
6:32	69–70
9:18–27	46
12:13–21	14
15:1–10	38
18:1–8	77
18:9–14	50
19:41	63
19:42	xix
24:13-32	53–54

John
4	37
9:1–17	36
16:33	151

Acts
2	8; 45
3:1–10	18–19

Romans
1:20	105–106
8:18–27	146
8:19, 21	105–106
8:19–24	103–104; 144–145
12:1–2	61
12:5	79–80
12:9–18	55

1 Corinthians
13:13	xix

2 Corinthians
5:16–21	100

2 Timothy
3:5	xvii

Hebrews
10:24	79–80; 126–127

James
1:17	69–70
1:17–27	43

Revelation
21:1	xix
21:1–4	103–104
22:1–2	105–106

www.ingramcontent.com/pod-product-compliance
Lightning Source LLC
Chambersburg PA
CBHW071502150426
43191CB00009B/1402